New Directions for
Community Colleges

Arthur M. Cohen
EDITOR-IN-CHIEF

Caroline Q. Durdella
Nathan R. Durdella
ASSOCIATE EDITORS

The Future of the Urban Community College: Shaping the Pathways to a Multiracial Democracy

Gunder Myran
Curtis L. Ivery
Michael H. Parsons
Charles Kinsley
EDITORS

Number 162 • Summer 2013
Jossey-Bass
San Francisco

The Future of the Urban Community College: Shaping the Pathways to a Multiracial Democracy
Gunder Myran, Curtis L. Ivery, Michael H. Parsons, Charles Kinsley (eds.)
New Directions for Community Colleges, no. 162

Arthur M. Cohen, Editor-in-Chief
Caroline Q. Durdella, Nathan R. Durdella, Associate Editors

New Directions for Community Colleges (ISSN 0194-3081, electronic ISSN 1536-0733) is part of The Jossey-Bass Higher and Adult Education Series and is published quarterly by Wiley Subscription Services, Inc., A Wiley Company, at Jossey-Bass, One Montgomery St., Ste. 1200, San Francisco, CA 94104. POSTMASTER: Send address changes to New Directions for Community Colleges, Jossey-Bass, One Montgomery St., Ste. 1200, San Francisco, CA 94104.

Subscriptions cost $89 for individuals in the U.S., Canada, and Mexico, and $113 in the rest of the world for print only; $89 in all regions for electronic only; $98 in the U.S., Canada, and Mexico for combined print and electronic; $122 for combined print and electronic in the rest of the world. Institutional print only subscriptions are $311 in the U.S, $351 in Canada and Mexico, and $385 in the rest of the world; electronic only subscriptions are $311 in all regions; combined print and electronic subscriptions are $357 in the U.S. and $431 in Canada and Mexico.

Editorial correspondence should be sent to the Editor-in-Chief, Arthur M. Cohen, at the Graduate School of Education and Information Studies, University of California, Box 951521, Los Angeles, CA 90095-1521. All manuscripts receive anonymous reviews by external referees.

New Directions for Community Colleges is indexed in CIJE: Current Index to Journals in Education (ERIC), Contents Pages in Education (T&F), Current Abstracts (EBSCO), Ed/Net (Simpson Communications), Education Index/Abstracts (H. W. Wilson), Educational Research Abstracts Online (T&F), ERIC Database (Education Resources Information Center), and Resources in Education (ERIC).

Microfilm copies of issues and articles are available in 16mm and 35mm, as well as microfiche in 105mm, through University Microfilms Inc., 300 North Zeeb Road, Ann Arbor, MI 48106-1346.

CONTENTS

EDITORS' NOTES   1
Gunder Myran, Curtis L. Ivery, Michael H. Parsons, Charles Kinsley

1. Overview: The Future of the Urban Community College   7
Gunder Myran, Michael H. Parsons
Leaders are called to transform the very nature of the urban community college just as those who came before them responded to the
social revolution of the 1950s and 1960s amid the civil rights movement of that era.

2. The Urban Crisis and Pathways to a Multiracial Democracy   19
Curtis L. Ivery
Realization of a multiracial democracy is challenged by color-blind
politics and postracial supposition, fueled in part by the election of our
first black President in 2008, but contradicted by the chronic persistence of racial segregation and social inequality.

3. A New Leadership Paradigm for the 21st Century   27
Calvin Woodland, Michael H. Parsons
Leadership in the 21st century will require new insights and models.
The authors blend theory and experience into a design for engaging
the "new normal" in higher education.

4. The Future-Shaping Function of the Governing Board   37
Rosemary Gillett-Karam
The unique relationship between boards and the urban colleges they
serve is examined from the perspective of a university professor who
also serves as a community college trustee.

5. The Employability Gap and the Community College Role in   45
Workforce Development
Gunder Myran, Curtis L. Ivery
Community colleges are becoming the primary source of middle-skill
talent through their workforce development programs. This chapter
explores the ways urban colleges are striving to close employability
and wealth gaps by linking workforce and social equity objectives.

6. Reframing Community Partnerships   55
Jerry Sue Thornton
This chapter frames innovative and creative ways to develop unique
partnerships with local high schools and employers, exemplified by
the best collaborative practices of Cuyahoga and other community
colleges.

7. Increasing the Relevance of Curricular and Student Services   63
in the Urban Community College
Eduardo J. Padrón
Like America itself, Miami Dade College's evolution as an institution of
multiracial democracy started out in reality as quite the opposite—
mostly segregated in the beginning, but now a national model of student diversity and success.

8. Achieving a Multiracial Democracy on Campus   75
Rufus Glasper
The goal of multiracial equity is not just a phrase in mission statements, but a top-down strategic necessity for community colleges
founded on and dedicated to the principles of social justice.

9. Capacity Building: Reshaping Urban Community College   85
Resources in Response to Emerging Challenges
Wright L. Lassiter, Jr.
Metropolitan community colleges face a myriad of convergent challenges. Sometimes to make sense of it all, it helps to think of an onion,
from the outer layers of support to inner core of instructional
services.

10. The New Community College Business and Finance Model   93
Gunder Myran
Community colleges are transitioning from an old business and finance
model to a new future-shaping one. They are being redesigned to
become leaner, smarter, more efficient, more creative, and more
focused in response to long-term financial constraints as well as rapidly
changing workplace skill requirements, technological advances, and
globalization.

INDEX   105

EDITORS' NOTES

This sourcebook is dedicated to the memory of Marliss Myran, who passed during its final completion but was always the primary object of devotion for her loving husband, Gunder.

The urban community college exploded onto the national higher education scene in the 1960s as Baby Boomers began to flood through its open doors and demands by minorities for equal access to educational and economic opportunity reached the boiling point. Early adopters of the community college idea in urban centers were Chicago, Los Angeles, and New York City. It was said at the time that a new community college (many still called junior colleges) was created every week. In fact, 413 were born during the 1960s, including start-ups in Cleveland, Dallas, St. Louis, Detroit, Miami, Denver, Phoenix, Philadelphia, and Seattle.

One of the early national meetings about the potential of the community college to energize urban change took place in Dallas in 1966. It involved the American Association of Junior Colleges (now the American Association of Community Colleges, or AACC) and urban community college representatives. The meeting resulted in a report entitled *The American Dream Updated,* which contained this statement: "We accept the challenge of the inner city with all its complexities, its difficult problems and immense costs. The battleground is in the inner city—stay and fight where you are."

But first another skirmish was in order, as no black community college president had served on the national association's board of directors prior to 1970. The board had previously added three new seats to accommodate minority representation, but the nominating committee failed to propose a single African American candidate. During a disruptive floor fight at the national convention in 1970, a caucus of African American presidents demanded a leadership voice in their own association. They proposed a complete slate of minority nominees for board positions, resulting in the election of Malcolm Hurst that year, followed by Norvel Smith in 1971. Another important milestone was the election of Abel Sykes as board chair in 1976. Since then, a number of African American and Latino presidents have served as board chairs and members.

Edmund Gleazer, AACC president from 1958 to 1981, led a Kellogg Foundation–funded effort during the early 1970s called Project Focus to democratize the association and national community college leadership. The Project Focus report in 1971 resulted in changes to the board structure

NEW DIRECTIONS FOR COMMUNITY COLLEGES, no. 162, Summer 2013 © 2013 Wiley Periodicals, Inc.
Published online in Wiley Online Library (wileyonlinelibrary.com) • DOI: 10.1002/cc.20053

and the inclusion of various administrative groups in the form of councils. One of the first was the National Council of Black American Affairs.

It can be well said that the current black chancellors and presidents of urban community colleges stand on the shoulders of those pioneers who came before them. A case in point is Walter Bumphus, AACC's current president and the first African American to hold that national leadership position. He joins the legacy of Hurst, Smith, Sykes, and others who helped make the dream of "democracy's college" come true at the highest national level.

Following decades of robust growth and cycles of financial ups and downs, today's community colleges are challenged to reinvent themselves once again—to do much more with less. They are called upon to maintain their cherished open-door and low-cost principles even while in many cases losing much of their state and local funding. They are expected to produce 50% more degree and certificate completions by 2020, although a third of the nation's high school graduates are not ready for college-level work. In addition to their traditional university transfer, student support, and general, career, continuing, and developmental education functions, they are looked upon as a primary source of workforce talent critical to the creation of a highly skilled and globally competitive labor force. And as postsecondary institutions in the best position to accommodate the various needs of an increasingly diverse and underprepared low-income citizenry, they are the country's beacon of hope for reversing the widening achievement, wealth, and opportunity gaps that threaten the very existence of an American middle class.

To all these challenges, known loosely and collectively as the "new normal," the editors of this sourcebook have one more to add: the unfinished business of a true multiracial democracy. This is not something new, but an ideal as compelling as those well-known words in the Declaration of Independence proclaiming the indisputable truth "that all men are created equal, that they are endowed by their Creator with certain unalienable Rights, that among these are Life, Liberty and the pursuit of Happiness." Multiracial democracy is not just "a goal for a nation founded on the principle of human equality" as defined throughout this volume, but the founding force behind community colleges. As the most important measure of their future success, it is also the ultimate motivation for the unfinished work of all community colleges.

Urban community colleges have been at the forefront of the quest for a multiracial democracy, serving as examples for each other as well as for suburban and rural colleges facing many of the same issues posed by rising poverty, declining college readiness, demographic transformation, dwindling financial resources, and greater workforce-training demands. Looking to the future, all share the commitment to increase student success, economic prosperity and social equity. It is in this spirit that we offer these stories, experiences, and best practices from urban colleges–to inspire all in their universal quest "to come together across lines of race, religion, class, and gender to collectively unite in support of racial and civic equality" (Ivery & Bassett, 2011, p. xcii).

The chapters of this sourcebook are organized under two primary themes. The first three essays outline dimensions of the future urban community college, while the remainder address the solutions that are already shaping the colleges of tomorrow.

Chapter 1 by Gunder Myran and Michael Parsons is a call to action for America's urban community colleges to redress massive and persistent disparities that have created a "pathology of despair" in our inner cities. It examines how national completion and success agendas can accomplish the goal of a multiracial democracy, and poses numerous dimensions for the future of these institutions. Chapter 2 by Curtis Ivery further discusses the history of racial identity and understanding and how it contributes to the urban condition of today. It then looks at the emerging consensus on effective ways to deal with the consequences. Chapter 3 by Calvin Woodland and Michael Parsons presents a new leadership paradigm for engaging the "new normal" of the 21st century, which is described in various ways throughout the book and defined in this chapter as "Today's seemingly bleak budget coupled with rapid, omnidirectional change."

In Chapter 4, Rosemary Gillett-Karam focuses on the unique relationship between trustees and the urban colleges they serve, from the perspective of a university professor who also serves as a Baltimore City Community College board member. Ten recommendations for future governance illustrate the importance of commitment to values and missions. In Chapter 5, Gunder Myran and Curtis Ivery discuss the new emphasis on workforce development as key to disrupting the cycle of poverty and unemployment that has produced a wealth gap of 2,000% between white and black households. Middle-skill careers in particular have become a niche area for community colleges, further described in terms of career education and workforce development innovations. Chapter 6 by Jerry Sue Thornton offers best-practice examples of community partnerships resulting in career training and employment opportunities for high school students at community colleges in Ohio and Missouri. The programs tend to emphasize high-demand STEM careers in fields such as the aerospace industry that typify tomorrow's opportunities for the future workforce.

Chapter 7 by Eduardo J. Padrón on increasing the relevance of curricular and student services tells the very American story of a community college in Miami that in its earliest years segregated most of its black and white students. Now Miami Dade College has grown into one of the country's biggest and most diverse institutions of higher education, and is one of three cadres working to produce national models for student success under partnership grants from the Gates Foundation's Completion by Design program. In Chapter 8, Rufus Glasper explains how Maricopa Community Colleges (also one of the nation's largest, with 200,000 credit and noncredit students at 10 geographically based colleges in the metro Phoenix region) has thoroughly infused its institutional culture with *strategic* diversity awareness and responsiveness during the past 20 years.

In Chapter 9, Wright Lassiter addresses capacity building, the process of reshaping community college resources in light of dwindling traditional revenue streams. After describing the "operational budget onion" as a vehicle for identifying and addressing budget and service priorities, this chapter delves into specific examples of managing deficits with improved cost efficiencies and programs like early retirement. Also described is the leveraging of information technology in federal financial aid applications to enhance service and improve student retention in the process. Finally, Chapter 10 by Gunder Myran urges community colleges to transition to a new business and finance model. The new model focuses on innovations that create new markets and program delivery methods while adapting to emerging financial constraints and changing demographic, economic, technological, and social conditions. Ultimately, the model orchestrates all college resources for maximum impact on student, business, and community goal achievement.

Gunder Myran
Curtis L. Ivery
Michael H. Parsons
Charles Kinsley
Editors

Reference

Ivery, C. L., & Bassett, J. A. (Eds) (2011). *America's urban crisis and the advent of color-blind politics: Education, incarceration, segregation, and the future of U.S. multiracial democracy*. Lanham, MD: Rowman & Littlefield.

GUNDER MYRAN is president emeritus of Washtenaw Community College in Ann Arbor, Michigan. Prior to his 23-year tenure as WCC's president, he served as a professor in administration and higher education in the College of Education at Michigan State University. He is also a faculty member and national advisory board member of the Doctorate in Community College Leadership at Ferris State University.

CURTIS L. IVERY has been chancellor of Wayne County Community College District in Detroit since 1995. For his work at WCCCD and numerous writings that include publication of America's Urban Crisis and the Advent of Color-Blind Politics in 2011, he has become a nationally recognized authority on urban affairs and the recipient of several awards acknowledging his service to community, higher education, and social equity.

NEW DIRECTIONS FOR COMMUNITY COLLEGES • DOI: 10.1002/cc

MICHAEL H. PARSONS *is visiting adjunct professor in the Community College Leadership Doctoral Program at Morgan State University in Baltimore. He retired as chief instructional officer and professor of education and sociology at Hagerstown Community College in Maryland.*

CHARLES KINSLEY *is an independent writer, editor, and publishing consultant who works frequently on community college issues. A graduate of Lansing Community College and Michigan State University, he is a former daily newspaper managing editor, news editor, copy editor, staff writer and bureau chief, and recent journalism instructor at Central Michigan University.*

NEW DIRECTIONS FOR COMMUNITY COLLEGES • DOI: 10.1002/cc

1

We view this New Directions for Community Colleges sourcebook as a call to action for America's urban community colleges to become leaders on the frontier of a genuine multiracial democracy. It is a call to redress massive and persistent disparities that have created what Cornel West refers to as the "pathology of despair" in our inner cities. Leaders are challenged to transform the very nature of the urban community college just as those who came before us responded to the social revolution of the 1950s and 1960s amid the civil rights movement of that era. Today's urban college is at the front line of the next phase in this revolution, leading efforts to overcome the persistent and entrenched racial, educational, economic, and social inequities that threaten the vitality of our cities and our nation's democratic principles. Suburban and rural community colleges have a stake in this same experience, as they also serve areas of increasing diversity and poverty.

Overview: The Future of the Urban Community College

Gunder Myran, Michael H. Parsons

Since the beginning of the civil rights movement in the 1950s, community colleges have been a primary educational pathway for persons from low-income and minority backgrounds to achieve the American dream by gaining access to the economic and social mainstream. Much has been accomplished by community colleges to resolve the nation's discriminatory past and achieve genuine equality, but we still have a long way to go.

Given the painfully evident realities of racial and economic disparities in American society, we are called to renew our commitment to the democratization of higher education and, indeed, our society. This calling is most urgent in our largest cities, where the failure of opportunity is most pronounced. With urban colleges in the lead, all must renew their commitment to the open door of educational opportunity and shape new pathways to a multiracial democracy. Only then, at long last, can the United States achieve the egalitarian ideals on which it was founded.

NEW DIRECTIONS FOR COMMUNITY COLLEGES, no. 162, Summer 2013 © 2013 Wiley Periodicals, Inc.
Published online in Wiley Online Library (wileyonlinelibrary.com) • DOI: 10.1002/cc.20054

Milieu of the Urban Community College

The term *urban community colleges* refers throughout this issue to those serving the largest metropolitan regions anchored by major urban hubs. In most cases, the service area includes a high-density urban center and related neighborhoods, an urban/suburban transition fringe, suburban areas, and limited rural areas. At the core of all, the community college operates in a milieu of despair and promise.

"In the nation's inner cities, the idea that we've entered a truly color-blind era that affords equal opportunity to all is a fantasy that ignores the reality of what for decades has been defined as the 'crisis in urban America'—generational conditions of concentrated poverty, unemployment, segregation, incarceration, inadequate education, and related ills, which have disproportionately afflicted African American, Latino, and non-white populations" (Ivery & Bassett, 2011, p. xvi).

Author Fred Pierce describes the paradox faced by all large cities. On one hand they are centers of racial and economic isolation, poverty, crime, drugs, family disintegration, failed schools, and dashed hopes. On the other, they are also economic powerhouses, cultural hubs, and drivers of social change (Pierce, 2010). In this turbulent environment, the urban community college offers the promise of a better future for individuals, businesses, and the communities it serves. It is a beacon of hope, a partner with other organizations in economic and social transformation.

Shaping the Pathways to a Multiracial Democracy

A multiracial democracy is a society in which people of all races, religions, classes, and genders unite in support of principles of social justice and racial and civic equality. It is a call for new ways to address long-term, unresolved racial inequities. It is a call to confront and dismantle at last the residual impact of legalized discrimination from the past. It is time to close the equity gap and achieve the yet-unfulfilled promise of equality for all.

As discussed further in Chapter 2 of this volume, the concept of a multiracial democracy started circulating in higher education about a decade ago "as a goal for a nation founded on the principle of human equality" (Ivery & Bassett, 2011, p. 133). Proponents reject "color blind" and "post-racial" ideologies that promote the erroneous idea that racial identity no longer has any meaningful influence on access to opportunity in the United States. Such views are wholly untethered from the reality of minorities who continue to suffer the consequences of uneven wealth, education, health care, incarceration, and other dimensions of American life (Ivery & Bassett, 2013). Certainly, there have been significant advances since the civil rights movement began 50 years ago; yet racial and ethnic identity continues to be the most socially relevant way to understand the persistent lack of opportunity and achievement today.

Community Colleges as Talent Centers for a Knowledge-Based Economy

Lou Glazer, president of Michigan Future Inc., said in a 2013 interview that the strongest and healthiest metropolitan centers in the United States have two characteristics: a knowledge-based economy and a highly educated, talented workforce (Glazer, 2013). Talent and human capital, he said, trump all other factors in determining the vitality of large cities. Of the knowledge-based jobs in areas such as health, education, professional and business services (including various forms of engineering), finance and insurance, and information services (including media and software), about half are "middle-skill" jobs that require an associate degree or certification but no baccalaureate-level preparation.

Urban community colleges are the primary delivery systems for careers in the health professions as well as criminal justice, fire protection, automotive services, computer information, homeland security, graphic design, manufacturing, veterinary technology, welding, hospitality services, and office information systems. Thus, the emerging role of the college in a multiracial democracy centers on social and economic equity by increasing the number of persons from low-income and minority backgrounds who participate in a knowledge-based economy requiring a highly educated and talented workforce. Chapter 5 of this sourcebook explores in more detail the role of community colleges as a primary local resource for developing the workforce of the future and advancing the regional and state economy.

Advancing Economic Equity and the College Completion Imperative

As gatekeepers to upward mobility and the American dream, educational leaders today bear a responsibility unlike any generation before, according to William E. Kirwan, chancellor of the University System of Maryland. He told the 2013 annual meeting of the American Council on Education that social equity is the most compelling aspect of the national college-completion imperative. But equity requires the greatest of improvement in dismal college participation and success rates for low-income and minority populations, he said:

> "No matter what level of college completion we are ultimately able to reach as a result of the ambitious national goals, if the gains come mostly from the higher- and middle-income classes, or are overwhelmingly white, or primarily offspring of college-educated parents, we will not be able to claim success. Indeed, we will have contributed to creating for the first time in our nation's history a permanent economic underclass" (Kirwan, 2013).

He noted that 85% of children from families in the highest income quartile complete a college degree, compared to less than 8% of children from families in the lowest income quartile. National data also demonstrate that those with college degrees earn significantly more over a lifetime while experiencing far less unemployment. And college credentials are becoming even more necessary than ever as an estimated two-thirds of future jobs will require education beyond high school.

The 2013–2016 strategic plan of the Lumina Foundation, a premier national advocate and supporter of efforts to increase student achievement in community colleges, notes that "the national demand for talent to power our economy and support our democracy is growing rapidly. The vast majority of that talent . . . will come overwhelmingly from low-income, first generation, older adults and students of color" (Lumina, 2013a, p. 3). The plan calls for closing a myriad of individual attainment gaps for lower-income persons, immigrants, minorities, and males. Calling such inequities an "intolerable situation" that "must be rejected on moral grounds given the increasingly severe consequences of not obtaining a postsecondary credential," the plan further contends that "America's democracy and its economy are ill-served by a system that fails to tap all of our talent" (Lumina, 2013b, p. 5).

Since the majority of students from low-income and minority backgrounds start their postsecondary education at a community college, and a significant share do so in large cities, it is clear how the urban college plays a crucial role as a gatekeeper for social equity.

The Urban Community College Student Profile

Of the approximately 1,000 public community colleges in the United States, 56 are coidentified as both urban and large city. In fall 2011, these colleges enrolled approximately 1.5 million credit students—21% of the 7 million in all community colleges, according to the Integrated Postsecondary Education Data System (IPEDS) of the U.S. National Center for Education Statistics. Credit enrollment at the urban components of the largest urban/metropolitan community college districts in 2011 were: City University of New York (6 colleges), 97,712; Los Angeles Community College District (6 colleges), 97,013; Maricopa Community Colleges (6 colleges), 96,642; Miami Dade College (8 campuses), 63,736; and Houston Community College (6 colleges), 63,015.

African Americans, Latinos, American Indians, and other minorities represent 34% of the national population; they account for 27% of students at America's 700 public baccalaureate institutions, 32% at all public community colleges, and 54% at urban community colleges. On many of those inner-city campuses, the percentage of students from racial minorities is as high as 90%. They often live in concentrated poverty tracts with a poverty rate of 40% or greater (compared to the national average of 15%). They were likely raised by their mother or a female relative with the father absent from the scene. The majority did not participate in early childhood or preschool programs. They probably attended low-performing public schools with a high school dropout rate of close to 50%. The majority of their male neighbors between the ages of 18 and 24 were unemployed dropouts who have been either in prison or involved with the court system.

Most students of urban community colleges are from areas of racial segregation and economic isolation, as outlined above. They lack financial resources, basic literacy, good study habits, time management, and other college-related skills, and require at least one developmental course to become college ready. They usually must balance academics with other life responsibilities such as family and work. Compared to their counterparts at suburban and rural community colleges, they are much less likely to complete an associate degree or certificate program; based on 2011 data from IPEDS, about 28% of all community college students complete their education within three years, whereas only 14% of students in urban community colleges do so.

Transformational Leadership: Shaping the Pathways to a Multiracial Democracy

Leaders of the nation's urban community colleges are hard at work replacing the "pathology of despair" with a college and career success model founded on the objectives of a multiracial democracy. They are taking bold initiatives, as described in the chapters of this sourcebook, in areas such as leadership, policy development, workforce development, community partnerships, curriculum and student services, campus-wide diversity initiatives, resource development, and new business and financial models. In so doing, they are reframing the very definition of "democracy's college" through a fierce commitment "to come together across lines of race, religion, class, and gender to collectively unite in support of racial and civic equality" (Ivery & Bassett, 2011, p. xcii).

Mission Statements Reveal New Emphasis on Service Continuum

Analysis of their mission, value, vision, and goal statements provides a more specific picture of how urban colleges are positioning themselves for the future. The mission statement is the most fundamental and enduring expression of why the college exists. It proclaims the difference it seeks to make in the community and world. The most common phrases and concepts in the organizational statements of today's urban colleges reflect greatest emphasis on student success, diversity, equity, access, world view, excellence, and workforce development.

A particularly salient example of a mission statement that embraces the spirit of multiracial democracy comes from San Jose City College (California), which strives to "effect social justice by providing open and equitable access to quality education and programs that prepare individuals for successful careers and active participation in a diverse, global society." Wayne County Community College District (WCCCD, Michigan) seeks to "empower individuals, businesses, and communities to achieve their goals through excellent and accessible services, culturally diverse experiences, globally competitive higher education, and career advancement programs." The mission of Central Piedmont Community College in North Carolina is to "advance the life-long educational development of students consistent with their needs, interests, and abilities while strengthening the economic, social, and cultural life of its diverse community."

One conclusion to be drawn from this analysis is a dual commitment to individual educational needs as well as the larger economic and social needs of communities served. These colleges provide a continuum of services from individual development on one end to community development on the other. Most programming along the continuum emphasizes one end or the other yet has an impact on both. For example, a workforce development program for unemployed individuals contributes to regional economic progress. In the past decade, the community development dimension has become more central to the mission of urban colleges in recognition of the synergy between economic success and human capital. It is thus now common in the mission, value, function and goal statements of community colleges to see references such as workforce development, market demands, community engagement, collaboration, partnerships, common future, common good, and strategic alignment.

Reimagining the Future

Imagine the year 2025 from a magic carpet looking down at one of our urban community colleges. What do we see? Who is being served? What teaching and learning methods are being used? Where is learning taking place? How is the college making a difference in the communities being served? How is it distinctive from other educational institutions in the community?

A starting point might be to think about probable conditions in 2025. We can be certain, for example, that the population will continue to become more diverse as we move toward a society with no race or ethnic group accounting for more than half the total. We can be quite sure that the nation's economy will depend on a highly educated and talented workforce. In that regard, we will have to address the fact that the minorities of 2013 will be the least prepared to compete in a global, knowledge-based economy. We can also be quite certain that our major metropolitan centers, such as New York City, Detroit, Miami, Chicago, Dallas, and Los Angeles, will be the anchors of their state and regional economies.

A number of national initiatives are designed to transform the way community colleges respond to questions of the future. Analyzed below are three such initiatives: the Lumina Foundation's *Goal 2025* student success

NEW DIRECTIONS FOR COMMUNITY COLLEGES • DOI: 10.1002/cc

agenda, the *Reclaiming the American Dream* initiative of the American Association of Community Colleges (AACC), and the 2006 national survey of changing open-door practices of community colleges sponsored by WCCCD and the COMBASE consortium, a national organization of community colleges committed to community-based education.

Lumina Foundation *Goal 2025*

The Lumina Foundation has awarded more than $500 million in grants targeted at all aspects of its primary objective, summarized most recently in *Goal 2025,* to produce a national postsecondary attainment rate of 60%, an increase from the current rate of 39%—or 23 million more Americans by 2025. To reach that goal, it has identified eight strategies within two major imperatives to be accomplished by 2016. These strategies are paraphrased as follows to bend them toward direct applicability to urban institutions:

Strategic Imperative 1: Mobilizing to Reach *Goal 2025*

- *Build a social movement.* Increase the number of community organizations and groups that actively support increased student completion and social equity.
- *Mobilize employers.* Increase support for the student completion and social equity agendas of employers, community schools and colleges, governmental agencies, media, nonprofit organizations, and other community-based groups.
- *Mobilize higher education.* Increase student success through evidence-based policies and practices that close achievement gaps for underserved students and improve overall completion rates.
- *Advance state-level policies* to increase student attainment and address achievement gaps for underrepresented populations.
- *Advance federal policy for increased attainment.*

Strategic Imperative 2: Creating a 21st-Century Higher Education System

- Design new models for student financial support.
- Design new higher education business and finance models.
- Design new systems for quality credentials defined by learning and competence, rather than time. Create clear learning pathways for students that are aligned with workforce needs and trends.

Reclaiming the American Dream (AACC)

The report of the AACC's 21st-Century Commission on the Future of Community Colleges presents seven recommendations for reimagining the future of community colleges within *three Rs—Redesign, Reinvent, Reset* (AACC, 2012, pp. viii-ix):

- *Redesign students' educational experiences*: Increase college completion rates by 50% by 2020, dramatically improve college readiness, and close the American skills gap.
- *Reinvent institutional roles*: Refocus to meet 21st-century education and employment needs, and invest in support structures to serve multiple colleges through collaboration.
- *Reset the system*: Target public and private investments, and implement policies and practices that promote rigor, transparency, and accountability for results.

Reinventing the Open Door

A national study of the changing open door of community colleges resulted in a 2006 conference sponsored by AACC, the COMBASE consortium, and WCCCD. It also led to the publication of *Reinventing the Open Door: Transformational Strategies for Community Colleges* (Myran, 2009). This publication identified four cornerstones of the new community college open door:

Student Access

- Strengthen community-based efforts to reach out to potential students, schools, and other community groups to instill awareness of the benefits of a community college education.
- Strengthen student-friendly admissions, orientation, financial aid, program selection, and other entry services.
- Strengthen support services that empower students to develop college- and career-readiness skills, such as basic literacy, study skills, and time management, thereby overcoming the barriers to college and career achievement.

Student Success

- Focus on the assessment of learning outcomes and evidence-based continuous improvement at the course, program, certificate, and associate degree levels.
- Create a college-wide completion initiative to increase the number of students who complete courses, programs, and credentials in line with their career and academic goals.
- Promote student engagement with faculty members and other students both in and outside the classroom.
- Focus on excellence of programs and services, creating a culture of evidence as it relates to student achievement and increasing the capacity of the college to meet the varied needs of diverse students.

Campuswide Inclusiveness

- Involve students, faculty, and staff in creating an accepting, affirming, and open environment with a shared sense of common purpose in which individuals can grow, give expression to their educational and career goals, and learn to live together in a multicultural global society.
- Expand diversity, equity, and multicultural programming to embrace differences in race, gender, ethnicity, religion, national origin, socioeconomic class, marital status, disabilities, sexual orientation, educational and experiential background, and other characteristics.
- Advance diversity training for faculty, staff and student leadership groups.

Community Engagement

- Engage the college governing board, executive leaders, faculty, and staff in community-based efforts to confront the very problems that cause barriers to student career and academic achievement, especially for low-income and minority students, such as unemployment, poverty, crime, drugs, and neighborhood disintegration.
- Expand service-learning programs, internships, work-study programs, and other community-based learning initiatives that benefit both the student and community.
- Engage in specific community problem-solving projects in partnership with other organizations in areas such as public school reform, adult literacy, and workforce development.

Tomorrow's Most Promising Alternatives

Given the above analysis of likely future societal trends and insights from national initiatives and studies, what are the most promising alternative futures of the urban community college? Consider some scenarios:

Open Door College.   In this scenario, the college focuses on the four cornerstones of the reinvented open-door philosophy: student access, student success, campuswide inclusiveness, and community engagement.

Completion College.   In this scenario, the college serves as primary educator and career-readiness center in cooperation with K–12 schools and other community organizations. It focuses on designing and implementing clear pathways for students that integrate all phases of their flow including the initial phases of community outreach, admissions, orientation, financial aid, and course registration; the early phases such as developmental education and college success programs; the primary phases of choosing and completing a program of study; and the final phases of completion and follow-up. In each phase, the assessment of student performance becomes the basis for data-informed continuous improvement efforts.

NEW DIRECTIONS FOR COMMUNITY COLLEGES • DOI: 10.1002/cc

Workforce Development College.   In this scenario, the college becomes the primary provider of a highly educated and talented community workforce in alignment with emerging regional workforce and economic development needs. It plays the primary matchmaking role, using "big data" or analytics to create the best possible match between workforce skills required by employers, the actual skills of those in the workforce, and skills offered by community colleges and other education institutions.

Social Equity College.   In this scenario, the college is a primary leader, advocate, and implementer of community-wide efforts to shape a multiracial democracy in which people of all races, religions, classes, and genders unite in support of new principles of social justice and racial equality. Expanding beyond educational programs, the college offers resources and expertise to actively pursuing solutions for the urban crisis in cooperation with community partners. As the center of intellectual capital, entrepreneurship and workforce development, it becomes the community conscience and champion. It is a catalyst for progress, engaging other leaders and citizens in transforming the city into inclusive and diverse centers of economic and cultural vitality.

"New Normal" College.   In this scenario, the community college has adapted to the "new normal" of limited financial resources, an increasingly diverse and needy student body, demands for increased accountability for producing results that justify the investment of public funds, and pressures to demonstrate excellence and effectiveness to accrediting agencies and governmental units. The new-normal scenario foresees a future of increased productivity, financial sustainability, and quality. Through program reviews and audits, program cost models and other financial controls, resources are orchestrated to produce maximum impact on student success and other high-priority goals.

Conclusion: Reframing "Democracy's College"

Wangari Maathai, recipient of the 2004 Nobel Peace Prize for her contribution to sustainable development, democracy and peace, stated that "In the course of history, there comes a time when humanity is called to shift to a new level of consciousness, to reach a higher moral ground. A time when we have to shed our fear and give hope to one another. That time is now."

Shifting to a new level of consciousness and a higher moral ground is a compelling call to arms for urban community colleges. How are they shaping their futures in the face of persistent and entrenched racial, educational, economic, and social inequities in our cities and society? The best future will no doubt be an amalgamation of the alternative scenarios outlined above. They will share with all community colleges dimensions of the open-door and completion scenarios, although advancing these will be more challenging in the urban environment where a higher percentage of students pose significant barriers to career and academic success. All share the realities of the new-normal scenario to varying degrees; the devastation of revenue streams during the recent economic crisis challenges them to achieve financial sustainability through cost controls and increased productivity. Distinctive dimensions of the future urban community college can be summarized as follows:

- *Serving the Individual and Public Good.* Mission statements indicate a trend toward the dual purposes of individual and community development.
- *Workforce Development.* Talent will trump all other factors of economic growth in central cities. The future urban community college will play a pivotal role in advancing the economic viability of the city and metropolitan region it serves through career and workforce education and other talent-development initiatives.
- *Linking Workforce Development to Social Equity.* The success of the urban community college in providing a highly educated and talented workforce depends on its ability to link this effort to social equity objectives. The capacity of students to attain their employment and career objectives will be greatly enhanced when the college and community achieve their social equity objectives. In the community, this means overcoming structural barriers to career and college readiness such as racial and economic isolation, poverty, and illiteracy; within the college, it is achieved by defining equity as the delivery of services to individual students according to the unique needs of each.

In these ways, the nation's urban community colleges will reframe the very definition of "democracy's college." Perhaps, in so doing, we can redefine the nature of democracy itself by finally becoming the society our founders dreamed that the United States would be.

References

American Association of Community Colleges (2012). *Reclaiming the American dream: Community colleges and the nation's future.* Washington DC. Retrieved from www.aacc.nche.edu/aboutcc/21stcenturyreport/21stCenturyReport.pdf

Glazer, L. (2013). *Stateside: Higher education at the core of Michigan's revival.* Michigan Radio (NPR). Retrieved from www.michiganradio.org/post/stateside-higher-education-core-michigans-revival

Ivery, C. L., & Bassett, J. A. (Eds.) (2011). *America's urban crisis and the advent of color-blind politics: Education, incarceration, segregation, and the future of U.S. multiracial democracy.* Lanham, MD: Rowman & Littlefield.

Ivery, C. L., & Bassett, J. A. (2013). Reclaiming integration and opportunity in the era of multiracial democracy. *Huffington Post,* March 6. Retrieved from www.huffingtonpost.com/dr-curtis-l-ivery/reclaiming-integration-and-opportunity_b_2814923.html

Kirwan, W. (2013). *The completion imperative: Harnessing change to meet our responsibilities.* Retrieved from www.acenet.edu/news-room/Pages/Kirwan-Addresses-Social-Equity-and-College-Completion-in-2013-Atwell-Lecture.aspx

Lumina Foundation (2013a). Strategic plan, 2013–2016: Executive summary. Retrieved from   www.luminafoundation.org/advantage/document/goal_2025/2013-Strategic _Plan-Executive_Summary.pdf

Lumina Foundation (2013b). Strategic plan, 2013–2016. Retrieved from www.lumina foundation.org/advantage/document/goal_2025/2013-Lumina_Strategic_Plan.pdf

Myran, G. (Ed.) (2009). *Reinventing the open door: Transformational strategies for community colleges.* Washington, DC: Community College Press, American Association of Community Colleges.

Pierce, F. (2010). *The coming population crash and our planet's surprising future.* Boston, MA: Beacon Press.

GUNDER MYRAN *is president emeritus of Washtenaw Community College in Ann Arbor, Michigan. Prior to his 23-year tenure as WCC's president, he served as a professor in administration and higher education in the College of Education at Michigan State University. He is also a faculty member and national advisory board member of the Doctorate in Community College Leadership at Ferris State University.*

MICHAEL H. PARSONS *is visiting adjunct professor in the Community College Leadership Doctoral Program at Morgan State University in Baltimore. He retired as chief instructional officer and professor of education and sociology at Hagerstown Community College in Maryland.*

2

Realization of a multiracial democracy is challenged like never before by a new era of color-blind politics and postracial supposition, fueled in part by the election of our first black President in 2008, but contradicted by the chronic persistence of racial segregation and social inequality.

The Urban Crisis and Pathways to a Multiracial Democracy

Curtis L. Ivery

The chapters of this book serve as an excellent framework for defining the future of urban community colleges as a primary mechanism for achieving multiracial democracy in America. Despite its transformation into a nation with a majority of minorities, the United States continues to be afflicted by significant and generational racial inequalities in economics, education, employment, incarceration, and other key areas of civic and social life. It is thus incumbent upon today's community college leaders to transform the very nature of our institutions, just as our predecessors were pioneers in response to social revolutions of the 1960s and 1970s. Though indeed we are decades removed from the open social and legal discrimination that defined previous eras, we remain as entrenched in the very conditions of inequality that gave rise to what is familiarly known across academic disciplines as "America's Urban Crisis" (i.e., urban underclass theory, Sugrue, 1986). But we now also confront new and emerging discourses of race and racial understanding that must be addressed if the philosophical intentions of the nation's democratic founding are to be fulfilled.

Multiracial Democracy: Origins and Definitions

Certainly, as community colleges engage the project of multiracial democracy, each will reflect the dynamics of race, class, gender, and immigration specific to their local areas and extended state geographies. This diversity

New Directions for Community Colleges, no. 162, Summer 2013 © 2013 Wiley Periodicals, Inc.
Published online in Wiley Online Library (wileyonlinelibrary.com) • DOI: 10.1002/cc.20055

of approaches is necessary to redress continuing inequalities on an institutional level. But it is also important to develop a common definition of multiracial democracy as a template for educational work and concise rationale in those communities that are unfamiliar with or skeptical of such a mission.

Influential work in this area was developed by noted sociologists Michael Omi and Howard Winant. Their important theory of "racial formation" (Omi & Winant, 1994, pp. 53–76) is critical to understanding how race functions in both social and political terms. A key point concerns what the authors identify as the "evolution of modern racial awareness" and "forces of racialization" that are influential in determining access to economic opportunity, education, and civic engagement.

Omi and Winant identify three major historical eras reflecting dominant "frames" (powell, 2009) of racial understanding. The first, in the 15th to 17th centuries during the seminal age of European colonialism, was characterized by the widespread view of racial identity as a religious/natural condition, manifested by God via Christianity and governed by the basic tenet that non-Europeans were not "full-fledged human beings" (Omi & Winant, 1994, p. 62).

The religious era of racial understanding developed in the 18th century, during the so-called Age of Enlightenment, into a "scientific" conception (Omi & Winant, 1994, p. 63). Racial identity was considered a biological condition with its own distinct permutations in intelligence, psychology, culture, and so forth, that could be discerned by scientific inquiry and empirical analysis. The third era of racial understanding, which takes root in the late 19th through 20th centuries, marks a crucial departure. It severs the concept of race from any religious or biological context, and locates it wholly within the social province of politics and language, where it has stood for decades across academic disciplines as the standard model/definition (Omi & Winant, 1994, pp. 64–65).

The recognition of race as a social-political construct represents a revolutionary turning point in the difficult and incomplete transition from slavery and legal discrimination to "multiracial democracy" (Omi & Winant, p. 66). Within this framework, we must consider the continuing salience of racial identity in context of the election and re-election of President Barack Obama. While certainly representing indisputable progress and *prima facie* evidence of early transformation into a multiracial democracy, Obama's political success has also been effectively utilized in the service of color-blind and postracial ideologies. These views presume that ample social equity has been achieved, and corrective measures like integration and affirmative action are therefore no longer necessary despite the abundance of glaring indications to the contrary. Of particular concern for urban community colleges are the ongoing resegregation of public schools and recent rulings of the U.S. Supreme Court that are likely to consolidate rather than alleviate worsening racial disparity.

NEW DIRECTIONS FOR COMMUNITY COLLEGES • DOI: 10.1002/cc

Resegregation Thwarts Progress

A conventional view of demographic transformation in the United States is that the increasing number of racial minorities is expected to form the new collective majority by outnumbering whites in the next 10–20 years and will naturally lead to greater racial integration in all areas of society. The premise of this view, reflecting the rationale of recent judicial rulings (*Parents*, 2007, et al.) is that since legal forms of discrimination in education, housing, employment, etc., have long been dismantled, there should be no barriers substantially preventing integration. To be sure, we have seen important gains in many areas, including housing, corporate hiring, and civic leadership. But at the same time we are also witnessing the disturbing emergence of new forms of racial discrimination (de Souza Briggs, 2005; and Krysan, 2002). This poses a direct threat to multiracial democracy, as the median wealth of white households in the United States is now 20 times that of African Americans and 18 times more than Latinos' (Reece & Holley, 2012, p. 3).

Meanwhile, minority presence in integrated schools has regressed substantially since the 1980s to levels where approximately 74% of African American and 80% of Latino students attend majority nonwhite schools with significant rates of poverty (Orfield, Kucsera, & Siegel-Hawley, 2012). Stanford University reports that nearly half of the almost 500 school districts that were under court order to desegregate as of 1990 have been released from judicial oversight during the past two decades, resulting in a slow but steady resegregation compared to districts where judicial oversight continues (Reardon, Grewal, Kalogrides, & Greenberg, 2011). Furthermore, the 2007 U.S. Supreme Court case, *Parents Involved in Community Schools v. Seattle School District*, which banned voluntary integration programs adopted by Seattle and Kentucky school districts, will likely exacerbate these dynamics (Ivery & Bassett, 2011).

The negative consequences of resegregation into poorer and richer school districts cannot be ignored, especially in consideration of a national student body that is nearly 50% nonwhite. Its implications are starkly evidenced by the lesser college readiness of urban students accounting for the lowest graduation rates of any postsecondary sector.

Toward a New Paradigm of Education

There are numerous approaches that community colleges can adopt in advancing multiracial democracy. Key areas include the philosophy of our governing boards, institutional leadership, community and educational partnerships, workforce development, curriculum, student services, voter registration, and the development of multicultural programs. At Wayne County Community College District (WCCCD) in Detroit, we have undertaken several initiatives that deserve mention. One is the establishment of an urban studies center (WCCCD Institute for Social Progress) that focuses

NEW DIRECTIONS FOR COMMUNITY COLLEGES • DOI: 10.1002/cc

on matters of racial segregation and educational inequality in the metro-Detroit area, which has long been one of the nation's most segregated regions. Our efforts have been supported by leading universities and civil rights institutes, including the Haas Diversity Research Center at Berkeley, the Kirwan Institute for the Study of Race and Ethnicity at The Ohio State University, Columbia University, and the University of Michigan.

We have also developed a specialized multicultural educational program through our urban institute that allows high school students to earn free college credit while studying in diverse classroom environments that would otherwise be unfamiliar via their highly segregated high schools. And we've engaged in numerous diversity programs, including the Diversity Advancement Project (Kirwan Institute/Center for Social Inclusion), to support efforts to improve racial inequalities in education, economics, and related areas.

Recently, we have allied with the American Association of Community Colleges in a national program called the Democracy Commitment Project, designed to respond to cyclical inequalities in education and employment afflicting low-income and communities of color. We have also partnered with the national organization, Opportunity Nation, to address issues of economic opportunity in our region (Ivery & Bassett, 2013).

Consensus Emerges from National Completion Initiatives

All of the above efforts can be reproduced in respective formats across the country. They reflect an important paradigm shift in the role of community colleges that is necessary in our unprecedented era of historical demographic transformation. Most encouraging in all major initiatives to increase student completions nationwide is an emerging consensus on the educational reforms necessary to economic and social vitality.

One such area of consensus is the need for more comprehensive data on how and why students succeed or fail. That includes *more* color-based data rather than less, as advocated by those who would remove race and ethnicity from all considerations, including government records, that might be used for affirmative action measures like remedial help for underprepared community college students. Rather than pretending gaps, inequities, and problems don't exist, we need more than anything to understand their nature in order to correct them.

This is especially relevant to the subject of remedial or developmental education that costs all public colleges and universities (meaning taxpayers) nearly $3 billion a year according to a 2008 report by the Delta Cost Project. Eighty percent is spent by community colleges with three times the number of undergraduates in remediation as four-year institutions (Delta Cost Project, 2008, pp. 10–12). Evidence of yet another gap exists in the rates of remediation by race—42% (the highest) for blacks compared to 31% (lowest) for whites. These data indicate how public schools are failing

NEW DIRECTIONS FOR COMMUNITY COLLEGES • DOI: 10.1002/cc

to adequately prepare more than a third of their graduates for college, and how the recent backlash against "special treatment" or remedial spending of any kind would have a particularly devastating impact on the number of otherwise disenfranchised students served by community colleges.

Nobody likes traditional remediation classes, least of all students who feel like instead of going to college they are paying to suffer through high school all over again. Developmental education can be so counterproductive, it may well account for the equally high dropout rate of those same students. Given the obvious need to somehow more effectively bridge the college and career readiness gap, community colleges are experimenting with new approaches such as imbedding developmental education in career education programs. Working more closely with high schools to get students on track for college as early as possible, through programs such as dual enrollment, is proving perhaps the best way to avoid remediation at the college level.

At WCCCD, we have also boosted our retention rates with an early alert intervention strategy that provides intrusive advising to developmental math and English as a second language (ESL) students. This advising model shows at-risk students that we care about their progress and success by proactively seeking them out *before* they get discouraged and quit. With such personal and persistent engagement, retention rates increased from 49% in 2006–2007 to 64% in 2009–2010, earning WCCCD national recognition as an Achieving the Dream Leader College in 2011.

CUNY's ASAP Garners Results and Accolades

An excellent example of the basic principle in intrusive (or disruptive) advising is its exponential expansion by City University of New York's Accelerated Study in Associate Programs (ASAP). Of special interest to urban colleges everywhere, CUNY has partnered with the New York City Department for Economic Opportunity to already *surpass* its goal of doubling the graduation rate for students earning associate degrees within three years.

Seventy percent of CUNY's 98,000 students at six borough community colleges are nonwhite. ASAP primarily targets those with low income who are most motivated to finish their education as soon as possible, but require one or two developmental courses first. It obligates participants to attend full-time, and comprehensively addresses numerous other obstacles to timely completion by waiving tuition for those who can't afford it, consolidating class schedules, combining cohorts with support faculty in smaller classes, and providing regular advisement, career preparation, tutoring, free transportation and textbook vouchers.

Six ASAP cohorts totaling 4,594 students were admitted from 2007 to 2012. In 2010, 55% of the 2007 cohort graduated, compared to 25% of a similar CUNY group not in the program:

As of September 2012, a second cohort of students admitted in fall 2009, of which 76 percent entered with 1–2 developmental needs, also realized a three-year graduation rate of 55 percent, versus 22.3 percent of comparison group students. The ASAP graduation rate is more than three times the national three year graduation rate of 16 percent for urban community colleges. (ASAP, 2013)

Kingsborough Community College in Brooklyn, which piloted ASAP at CUNY, was named a finalist-with-distinction for the 2013 Aspen Prize for Community College Excellence. The Aspen Institute cited cc for outstanding achievement in four areas: student learning outcomes, degree completion, labor market success in securing good jobs after college, and facilitating minority and low-income student success.

In a cost-benefit analysis to determine whether graduation gains are worth the added expense of ASAP, Columbia University Teachers College's Center for Benefit-Cost Studies of Education concluded in 2012 that it is so much more effective per graduate, the end result is "comparable to or less than that of the traditional approach. ASAP can increase considerably the number of CUNY community college graduates while actually reducing costs" (Levin, Garcia, & Morgan, 2012, p. 3).

By spending more on ASAP to produce more completions, the cost per completion would decrease by $6,500 "because its proportionately added effectiveness in degree production exceeds the added costs" (Levin, Garcia, & Morgan, 2012, p. 21).

Grappling with a New Era of Racial Repression

More data from promising best practices may also shed light on one of the most perplexing questions at the back of all discussions regarding racial equality: Why do so many minorities, particularly blacks, continue to lag so far behind whites? Legalized discrimination has been largely eliminated, and significant progress in achieving social equity has been made in the past 50 years. But the legacy of systematic repression is not so easily or quickly exorcized from culture, behavior, and attitudes. Thus, a disproportionate number of blacks are still relegated to segregated areas of extreme poverty, are locked up in prison at six times the rate of whites, and in effect are denied the basic entitlement of equal education for all.

As an educator, urban resident, and black father, I am passionate about addressing one of the most troubling aspects of the urban crisis: the status of black males and the devastating impact of absent fathers on African American families. In cities like Detroit, where an unusually high percentage of black children grow up never knowing their fathers, and across the country where the fatherless-home rate is three times higher for blacks than whites, the crisis is pervasive and only getting worse. Black communities and families have thrived throughout history and in many cases still do today. I have a warm place in my heart for the single women who heroically and successfully raise children even without a strong male presence. However, without fathers to serve as role models, providers, and equal partners in the family unit, the core of African American life will continue to disintegrate, to the detriment of our children and society.

Conclusion: Turning the American Dream into Reality

Community colleges are not about welfare or the abdication of personal responsibility. They represent the opposite, very American ideals of legitimate self-sufficiency, hard work, economic success, and good citizenship. As open-door institutions, we can create a welcoming, accepting, and learning-centered environment for our students. We can enable them to feel respected and valued in a highly structured learning environment for perhaps the first time in their lives. And ultimately, we can empower them to achieve their career, academic, and other life goals by creating and capitalizing on every opportunity for engagement throughout their educational experience.

Clearly, access alone is simply not enough anymore; we have already made great strides toward that most important first step of the American dream. We must now advance the student success agenda, thereby turning the dream into reality for those who have no one else to show them the way.

References

Accelerated Study in Associate Programs (ASAP), City University of New York. Retrieved from www.cuny.edu/academics/programs/notable/asap/about.html

de Souza Briggs, X. (Ed.) (2005). *The geography of opportunity: Race and housing choice in metropolitan America*. Washington, DC: The Brookings Institution.

Delta Cost Project (2008). *Diploma to nowhere*. American Institutes for Research. Retrieved from www.deltacostproject.org/resources/pdf/DiplomaToNowhere.pdf

Ivery, C. L., & Bassett, J. A. (Eds.) (2011). *America's urban crisis and the advent of color-blind politics: Education, incarceration, segregation, and the future of U.S. multiracial democracy*. Lanham, MD: Rowman & Littlefield.

Ivery, C. L., & Bassett, J. A. (2013). Reclaiming integration and opportunity in the era of multiracial democracy,. *Huffington Post*, March 6. Retrieved from www.huffingtonpost.com/dr-curtis-l-ivery/reclaiming-integration-and-opportunity_b_2814923.html

Krysan, M. (2002, November). Whites who say they'd flee: Who are they and why would they leave. *Demography, 39*(4).

Levin, H., Garcia, E., & Morgan, J. (2012, September). Cost-effectiveness of Accelerated Study in Associate Programs (ASAP) of the City University of New York (CUNY). Center for Benefit-Cost Studies of Education, Columbia University Teachers College. Retrieved from www.cuny.edu/academics/programs/notable/asap/Levin_Report_WEB.pdf

Omi, M., & Winant, H. (1994). *Racial formation in the United States: From the 1960s to the 1990s*. New York, NY: Routledge. (See also D. Martinez HoSang, O. LaBennett, & L. Pulido, Eds. (2012). *Racial formation in the 21st century*, Berkeley, CA: University of California Press).

Orfield, G., Kucsera, J., & Siegel-Hawley, G. (2012, September). *E Pluribus ... separation: Deepening double segregation for more students.* Los Angeles, CA: Civil Rights Project/UCLA.

Parents Involved in Community Schools v. Seattle School District No. 1, 551 U.S. 701 (2007); *Bartlett v. Strickland,* 129 S. Ct. 1231 (2009); and *Ricci v. DeStefano,* 557 U.S. (2009) are all recent cases advancing color-blind jurisprudence.

powell, j. (2009). *Talking about race: Towards a transformative agenda.* Columbus, OH: The Kirwan Institute for the Study of Race and Ethnicity at The Ohio State University.

Reardon, S. F., Grewal, E., Kalogrides, D., & Greenberg, E. (2011, December). *Brown fades: The end of court-ordered school desegregation and the resegregation of American public schools.* Stanford, CA: Stanford University Center for Education Analysis. Retrieved from http://cepa.stanford.edu/content/brown-fades-end-court-ordered-school-desegregation-and-resegregation-american-public-schools

Reece, J., & Holley, D. (2012, September). *Detroit at a crossroads: Emerging from crisis and building prosperity for all.* Columbus, OH: Kirwan Institute for the Study of Race and Ethnicity at The Ohio State University.

Sugrue, T. (1986). *The origins of the urban crisis: Race and inequality in postwar Detroit.* Princeton, NJ: Princeton University Press.

Additional Resources

Fuss, D. (1989). *Essentially speaking: Feminism, nature, and difference.* New York, NY: Routledge. This book offers an early overview of the critical development of the concept of race as a social construction.

Pew Research Center (2011, July 26). *Wealth gaps rise to record highs between whites, blacks, Hispanics.* Retrieved from www.pewsocialtrends.org/2011/07/26/wealth-gaps-rise-to-record-highs-between-whites-blacks-hispanics/

CURTIS L. IVERY has been chancellor of Wayne County Community College District in Detroit since 1995. For his work at WCCCD and numerous writings that include publication of America's Urban Crisis and the Advent of Color-Blind Politics in 2011, he has become a nationally recognized authority on urban affairs and the recipient of several awards acknowledging his service to community, higher education, and social equity.

NEW DIRECTIONS FOR COMMUNITY COLLEGES • DOI: 10.1002/cc

3

Leadership in the 21st century will require new insights and a new paradigm. With nearly 100 years of combined experience in community college teaching and administration, the authors of this chapter blend theory and experience into a design for engaging the "new normal."

A New Leadership Paradigm for the 21st Century

Calvin Woodland, Michael H. Parsons

If change is the constant of the 21st century, how will community colleges engage the "new normal?" The term has been used in many ways lately; perhaps the most precise definition as it relates to higher education is from the Lumina Foundation: "Today's seemingly bleak budget coupled with rapid, omnidirectional change" (Lumina, 2010, p. 1). The president of Mercer Community College in New Jersey, Patricia Donohue, suggests several imperatives for meeting the challenges:

> A national issue in higher education is leadership development—preparing the pipeline to fill the executive positions. As we face the "new normal" with limited funding, leaner staffing and success measured by outcomes (not inputs,) community colleges are expected to do more, serve more students and assure greater success and completion for our students. We must plan and operate strategically to accomplish these goals with lean staffing and leadership at all levels. (Donohue, 2011, p. 6).

There is little to argue with in her statement. What needs attention is the nature of the paradigm for achieving her goals. Significant research and discussion regarding which process will produce the greatest success has resulted in a common theme permeating all of it: Community colleges will look to their presidents for direction and motivation.

Several studies stand out in the process of determining direction. We will examine each and reflect on how their insights help leaders design

New Directions for Community Colleges, no. 162, Summer 2013 © 2013 Wiley Periodicals, Inc.
Published online in Wiley Online Library (wileyonlinelibrary.com) • DOI: 10.1002/cc.20056

strategies for the "new normal." For example, support for presidents' responsibilities comes from Hines, retired president of Spoon River College in Illinois. His model for moving from good to great identifies four variables that characterize great institutions:

"*Patience* includes objective measures"
"*Impact* involves identifying what would happen if the institution did not exist"
"*Resilience* refers to the ability of an institution to survive difficult times"
"*Longevity* requires that an organization sustain all of the other variables ..."
(Hines, 2011, p. 79)

In other words, presidents need a variety of skills to accomplish their task. Hines's variables are universal to all community college settings, and part of the coaching process provided by Achieving the Dream Inc., a national nonprofit dedicated to helping more community college students, particularly low-income students and those of color, stay in school and earn a certificate or degree.

How HECTIC Is It?

At the end of the opening decade of the 21st century, Margaret A. Miller, editor of *Change: The Magazine of Higher Learning*, summarized a series of articles on leadership. She identified six core competencies—forming the acronym HECTIC—that are essential for the emerging cadre of new leaders: humility, enthusiasm, charm, tenacity, integrity, and courage (Miller, 2010, p. 11). She concluded by stating that "... it seems that leaders these days need to be higher up the evolutionary scale than those guys who think that their job is simply to run things." She optimistically observed, however, that "... we're raising our successors right—that is, to be better than us."

Faculty from Morgan State University's Community College Leadership Doctoral Program designed a questionnaire based on Miller's competencies to conduct a pilot assessment (Parsons, 2012, pp. 1–7). Three former and two current community college presidents completed the questionnaire. The top three competencies in order of importance were integrity, courage, and enthusiasm. There was a tie for the least important elements—humility and charm. In effect, substance was essential, outweighing likability or impressions in the minds of all five experienced practitioners. Readers might examine the community college in which they work to ascertain the relevance of the competencies and determine how change-capable their culture is.

Adapting through Constructive Ambiguity

Miller's view of the leadership paradigm that 21st-century presidents must develop is anecdotal, derived from a series of case studies published in the

Change magazine. One of the nation's most insightful community college leaders, Belle Wheelan, reinforces Miller's perspective. In her nine years as president of two very different Virginia community colleges, Wheelan developed a template for success. It ranges from personal support systems to dealing with ambiguity, the latter by "understanding situations in the context of limited information" through efficient decision making, ethical behavior, a commitment to excellence, honesty, careful use of influence, the ability to laugh, patience in frustrating situations, and respect for all (Wheelan, 2012, pp. 26–27). Presidents must function as role models to engender a new commitment to the mission of the college. Adaptability is especially critical in an urban setting like Washington, D.C., due to the greater diversity of underprepared students requiring services tailored specifically to their individual needs.

Managing Change: What Is Truly Essential?

The process of identifying essential elements for organizational change is demanding. Matheny and Conrad (2012) synthesized a number of models that have proven successful in many Wisconsin two-year colleges. They identified three elements for planning and implementing change. These elements have greater utility in urban institutions, like Milwaukee Area Technical College (45% minority enrollment), than in some of the state's smaller, more homogeneous institutions (Matheny & Conrad, 2012, pp. 117–123):

- Understanding the source and locus of change is a critical first step in determining which strategies will be most effective for advancing partnerships with appropriate institutional support.
- Employ political and movement models to translate private organizational challenges into public issues. Through outreach and dialog with other similar organizations, the silent internal problems can find voice and spur change.
- Ensure the frequency and quality of interaction between stakeholders and college faculty and staff, recognizing that internal changes can be expedited and enhanced from external pressures. Effectively engaging external partners will help the college recognize the need for change and result in less drastic organizational shifts.

At the forefront of the quest for a true multiracial democracy, presidents of urban community colleges must strive to overcome entrenched and persistent disenfranchisement, lack of equity, and failure to engage the entire spectrum of need. For example, the University of the District of Columbia Community College (UDC-CC) in Washington serves six wards with a child poverty rate of 27% to 48%—two to three times the national average of 15%—and two other wards with a child poverty rate as low as

2% in one of the nation's wealthiest cities overall. With 5,500 students in just its fourth year of operation, UDC-CC's governing board has directed the president to concentrate primarily on the three poorest wards where the need for affordable postsecondary education is greatest.

The Nature of Disequilibrium

The conflict, chaos, and confusion of change that characterize the 21st century present a special challenge for community colleges. Various elements of the institution tend to be "out of synch" depending on the level of challenge. Two important processes of institutional effectiveness add a sense of direction to the maelstrom. The first is to "seek broad engagement in the development of evaluative processes and practices. Get as much faculty and frontline staff participation as possible to gain support and ownership of the process. This should not be a top-down process driven by administrative agendas" (Mulkins-Manning, 2011, p. 20). The second point reinforces the first: "If faculty and staff are expected to use results to improve programs and services, administrators need to read and respond to the reviews and evaluations in an honest and supportive way" (Mulkins-Manning, 2011). The result is likely to be stakeholder commitment to change as an ongoing commitment to quality of service. At UDC-CC, midmanagers highlight unit achievements monthly so the president and his leadership team can articulate accomplishments to external stakeholders.

The People as Leaders

The culture of adaptation depends on human collaboration. Much more discussion than real action has taken place to flatten the managerial pyramid. But successful future leaders will surround themselves with highly competent colleagues given authority commensurate with their responsibility. Senge, among others, suggests that "team learning will draw upon organizational diversity to generate creative strategies for engaging change" (Senge, 2006, p. 219).

The process requires distribution of authority and responsibility across the organization. New strategies are analyzed and an assessment design is adopted. Dissent and divergence are encouraged to avoid "group think." Finally, strategies need to be adopted that create an integrated service delivery system for diverse clients. The system must be characterized by open communication, expediting of regulation and procedure reform, and integration of institution-wide change (Wells, 2009, p. 81).

The Human Side of Adaptation

Given the multiplicity of heavy demands, it is of equal importance for modern community college leaders to develop balance in their lives. George Boggs, president of the American Association of Community Colleges from

2000–2010, suggests that "Because of time commitment, presidents often have difficulty in balancing their professional, private, and spiritual lives" (Boggs, 2011, pp. 3–22). He urges presidents to balance their many challenges equally because each "presents opportunities for leaders to strengthen their colleges and thereby the communities they serve" (Boggs, 2011, pp. 3–22).

Finally, Goleman's model for emotional intelligence (Goleman, Boyatzis, & McKee, 2004) encourages revealing the vulnerable side of one's personality and developing a way to release the tensions of leadership in a positive way to develop trust within the leadership team.

Any college leader must also evidence empathy and compassion for diverse stakeholders. Specific skills ensure that personnel are competent in dealing with ethnic, gender, age, and lifestyle differences. Hines offers 22 key ideas about leadership in community colleges. All have merit; number 8, for example, is an excellent synthesizing statement: "You are the leader, and people should look to you as a role model. Be sensitive to what you are modeling and whether it will serve others and the college well" (Hines, 2011, pp. 82–83).

Engaging a Changed Mission

When President Obama challenged community colleges in 2010 to produce 5 million (50%) more associate degrees and certificates by 2020, the mission of the "people's college" changed from open access to expanded success. College leaders need to embrace this change in a broader and deeper way. The final section of this chapter examines the integration of new leadership strategies to meet Obama's challenge while maintaining the viable elements of the community college's historic mission.

The Association of Community College Trustees (ACCT) recognized the need to assist leadership in the process by supporting development of an "initiative focusing on helping community college leaders understand what is transpiring on their campuses and to create a culture of data-informed decision making that leads to *measurable* and *meaningful* improvements in student success" (McClenney & Mathis, 2011, p. 7).

Following the recommendations made by these authors, the nonprofit educational research firm WestEd conducted a follow-up review of their findings. The conclusion suggests that while some action has been taken, much more is needed. "Boards can help move the agenda forward by making student success an explicit and deliberate priority, working with those both inside and outside of the institution to improve opportunities for students to be successful" (WestEd, 2012, p. 7).

Implementing the Promise of the Open Door

All of the researchers consulted share a common focus—an examination of what is known about achieving institutional transformation. From varying perspectives, they identify the need for taking action while just as genuinely reflecting upon results. Finally, they recognize that "Community colleges must redouble their efforts to demonstrate the passion, the 'fire in the belly,' to be a primary education resource and advocate for the poorest and disenfranchised" (Myran, 2009, p. 11). The drivers of institutional transformation must be accompanied by "a continuous review of the outcomes we measure including the opportunity to stretch to more dynamic outcomes" (Donohue, 2011, p. 6). "Acknowledging new or more successful outcomes and those who helped create them generates innate rewards and personal satisfaction, and models leadership behavior for others" (Donohue, 2011, p. 7). In essence, change is a journey rather than a destination unto itself.

The Utility of Synergy

Leadership is challenged to provide continuous direction. As Kanter succinctly states: "The fundamental task of leaders is to develop confidence in advance of victory in order to attract the [commitment] that makes victory possible—money, talent, support, empathy, attention, effort [and] people's best thinking" (Kanter, 2004, p. 87). In other words, the president personifies the college and works assiduously to attract commitment.

The next step is to create a climate of open discussion. Change is characterized too often by fear and resistance among those who perceive that it will somehow jeopardize their interests. Thus, innovation must be encouraged, data regarding outcomes disseminated widely, disagreement tolerated and active participation in problem-solving promoted. Lussier and Achua observe that the president must perform two roles successfully—disturbance-handler and negotiator. The roles must function collaboratively and be allocated throughout the leadership team as appropriate. The result is a transparency that builds trust (Lussier & Achua, 2013).

Change-Supporting Strategies

ACCT identifies a design that reduces the stress and fear produced by omnidirectional change. Two specific strategies are essential; one ensures that professional development and incentives are provided for senior administrators, faculty, and staff. The plan must be strategically aligned with the college's student success agenda. The other strategy cultivates "a common language, understanding and knowledge providing opportunities for practices to become routine throughout the institution" (ACCT, 2011, p. 14). These strategies are effective in making change a constant throughout the organization's culture and therefore less threatening.

The design is described as a framework for improving academic quality, closing achievement gaps, and improving student success. An integral aspect of the new style is suggested by Lussier and Achua: As final resource allocator, the president can reward success and encourage innovation to create the needed climate for change (Lussier & Achua, 2013, p. 15).

Conclusion: Reframing Community College Leadership

America is undergoing unprecedented and uneven change. To continue making progress toward greatness, resistance to affirming the equity of gender, ethnicity, lifestyle, and status must be confronted. In "vast areas of the United States, particularly in the inner cities, the idea that we've entered a truly color-blind era that affords equal opportunity for all is a fantasy that ignores the reality of what has for decades been defined as the 'crisis in urban America'" (Ivery & Bassett, 2011, p. xvi). Generational conditions of concentrated poverty, unemployment, segregation, incarceration, inadequate education, and related ills disproportionally affect so many African American, Latino, and nonwhite populations that urban community colleges are quite literally the only organizations offering any real hope of long-term solutions in the form of higher education increasingly necessary to individual success and prosperity. Even with limited resources, the "peoples' colleges" are ideally positioned to lead the attack on the status quo. "The choice of whether we continue to live as two nations, separate and unequal, is ours" (Ivery & Bassett, 2011, p. 165). Future generations and the critical viability of cities they live in deserve change now.

Myran makes it clear that community colleges face an arduous task in upgrading their mission and performance. "Ultimately, community college leaders must create a culture of learning and success in which all institutional programs, services, structures, and processes are oriented toward and judged by their effect on learning" (Myran, 2009, p. 47). As change expands and increases in rate, leaders must demonstrate a determination to integrate it into their institutional culture. To do so, Bolman and Gallos (2011) present a new vernacular for the role of leaders by describing them as analysts and systems designers. The authors summarize the operational parameters of these roles using *three Ps* for patience, persistence, and process. It is worthwhile to examine change in America's community colleges through this new lens:

Patience: Leaders must recognize that change comes slowly, especially in higher education. Balance is essential to avoid moving too fast and thus losing stakeholder support, or moving too slow to meet the changing needs of dynamic service areas. Bolman and Gallos (2011) counsel careful monitoring to identify critical timing and incidents that allow change to be perceived as normal, even desirable.

Persistence: Institutions cannot productively evolve by trying once then giving up. A strategy that assesses timing to introduce or reintroduce new ideas or operations has power in environments characterized by omnidirectional, rapid change. Stakeholders need time to process the potential change, and leaders need time to respond to inevitable problems and disagreements.

Process: Each organization's culture has a perceived correct way of doing things. If any proposed change is introduced in a way that allows stakeholders to see that it is consonant with "the way things are done around here," acceptance is more likely. A well-designed new process compatible with the organization's cultural norms attracts support and gradually defuses the chronic naysayers (Bolman and Gallos, 2011, pp. 75–76).

References

Association of Community College Trustees (ACCT) (2011). *Making good on the promise of the open door*.

Boggs, G. R. (2011, Winter). Community colleges in the spotlight and under the microscope. In J. J. Prihoda (Ed.), *New directions for community colleges: Presidents and analysts discuss contemporary challenges*. San Francisco, CA: Jossey-Bass.

Bolman, L. G., & Gallos, J. V. (2011). *Reframing academic leadership*. Hoboken, NJ: John Wiley & Sons, Inc.

Donohue, P. C. (2011). New normal needs leadership at all levels. In *Great leadership: Leading the new normal in community colleges*. Detroit, MI: Wayne County Community College.

Goleman, D., Boyatzis, R. E., & McKee, A. (2004). *Primal leadership: Learning to lead with emotional intelligence*. Boston, MA: Harvard Business Press.

Hines, T. E. (2011, Winter). Leadership: A balancing act. In J. J. Prihoda (Ed.), *New directions for community colleges: Presidents and analysts discuss contemporary issues*. San Francisco, CA: Jossey-Bass.

Ivery, C. L., & Bassett, J. A. (2011). *America's urban crisis and the advent of color-blind politics: Education, incarceration, segregation, and the future of U.S. multiracial democracy*. Lanham, MD: Rowman and Littlefield.

Kanter, R. M. (2004). *Confidence: How winning and losing streaks begin and end*. New York: Crown Business.

Lussier, R. N., & Achua, C. F. (2013). *Leadership: Theory, application, and skill development*. Mason, OH: South-Western, Cengage Learning. Retrieved from www.cengagebrain.co.nz/content/9781133895268.pdf

Lumina Foundation (2010). Navigating the "new normal." Indianapolis, IA: Lumina Foundation National Productivity Conference.

Matheny, C. J., & Conrad, C. (2012, Spring). A framework and strategies for advancing change and innovation in two-year colleges. In L. A. Phelps (Ed.), *New directions for community colleges: Advancing the regional role of two year colleges*. San Francisco, CA: Jossey-Bass.

McClenney, B., & Mathis, M. (2011). *Making good on the promise of the open door: Effective governance and leadership to improve student equity, success, and completion*. Washington, DC: Association of Community College Trustees.

Miller, M. (2010). The new leader. *Change: The Magazine of Higher Learning*, 2010.

Mulkins-Manning, T. (2011, Spring). Institutional effectiveness as process and practice in the American community college. In R. B. Head (Ed.), *New directions for community college: Institutional effectiveness*. San Francisco, CA: Jossey-Bass.

Myran, G. (Ed.) (2009). *Reinventing the open door: Transformational strategies for community colleges*. Washington, DC: The American Association of Community Colleges, Community College Press.

Parsons, M. (2012). *Assessment, presidential leadership and the 21st century*. Unpublished presentation. Philadelphia, PA: The League for Innovation in the Community College.

Senge, P. M. (2006). *The fifth discipline: The art & practice of the learning organization* (revised ed.). New York, NY: Doubleday, Inc.

Wells, C. (2009). Reinventing student services for today's diverse students. In G. Myran (Ed.), *Reinventing the open door: Transformational strategies for community colleges*. Washington, DC: The American Association of Community Colleges, Community College Press.

WestEd. (2012). Memorandum: What is the role of community college boards of trustees in student success initiatives? San Francisco, CA: Completion by Design.

Wheelan, B. (2012, April 5). 10 qualities of a strong community college leader. In *The Community College Journal*. Washington, DC: The American Association of Community Colleges.

CALVIN WOODLAND *is interim president of the four-year-old University of the District of Columbia Community College in Washington, D.C. Before that he was faculty member, counselor, dean, vice-president, and president at Capital Community College in Hartford, Connecticut.*

MICHAEL H. PARSONS *is visiting adjunct professor of community college leadership at Morgan State University in Baltimore. He has also been a faculty member, director of community services, and for 20 years chief instructional officer at Hagerstown Community College in Maryland.*

New Directions for Community Colleges • DOI: 10.1002/cc

4

Prevailing research tends to narrow the starting view of most authors, including those who write about community colleges and their governing boards in common terms of organizational structure, management style, roles and responsibilities, personality issues, and so forth. But this essay focuses more on one particular topic: the unique relationship between boards and the urban colleges they serve, from the perspective of a university professor who also serves as a community college trustee.

The Future-Shaping Function of the Governing Board

Rosemary Gillett-Karam

Pockets of populations form in cities divided by race and socioeconomic status. Sometimes railroad tracks or highways further separate and isolate these populations. In Baltimore, the surrounding "beltway" of Interstate 695 divides the mostly black city from the mostly white outlying county. One has the Community College of Baltimore County, with three campuses and four extension centers serving 29,000 students who are 48% white and 38% black. The other has Baltimore City Community College, with one main campus and 88 satellite sites (including churches, public libraries, businesses, and schools) for 7,100 students who are 76% black and 8% white.

The two institutions are more different than the 8 miles between them might suggest, evidenced most clearly by a graduation rate for the county college that is three times higher than the urban college with a greater proportion of minorities, recent immigrants, working single parents and underprepared, first-time college students from low-income families. In them, a special mission is revealed for governing boards that recognizes not only the race and socioeconomic status of students but also expresses an almost missionary call to representation and equity.

The success gap between urban and rural, white versus minority, wealthier versus poorer populations is but one of many that are typical across the higher education and community college spectrum. In general, the more urban the college, the lower the graduation rate, which

NEW DIRECTIONS FOR COMMUNITY COLLEGES, no. 162, Summer 2013 © 2013 Wiley Periodicals, Inc.
Published online in Wiley Online Library (wileyonlinelibrary.com) • DOI: 10.1002/cc.20057

predictably rises with distance from the inner city. In the past, many metro institutions believed they only had to mimic the missions and visions of more conventional colleges and universities. Now, however, they are committed to redressing the issues of urban decline by teaching, training, and finding success for their cultures of want.

Opportunity and Values Define Governance

Since the Truman Commission Report in the 1940s, community colleges have focused on giving underrepresented groups a chance to attend the "people's college." They reinforced postwar democracy by educating a new, nontraditional student body that included returning soldiers from World War II.

Opportunities also eventually arose for new governing board members to reflect a more diverse representation of society. Even though their numbers today still do not reflect their presence in American society, more women, blacks, Hispanics, and Asians are filling roles as board members, especially at urban community colleges. Throughout the United States, about 22% of all community college board chairs are women and about 22% are racial and ethnic minorities (Polonio, 2011, p. 21). Nationally, 60% of trustees are political appointees, and 40% are elected.

In the past 40 years, student demographics and governing boards alike have obviously become more diverse, especially at larger urban institutions. For example, Miami-Dade in Florida and San Antonio (Alamo district) in Texas now have a *majority* of Hispanic board members, while Baltimore City Community College has a majority of African American board members. In Houston, the majority of board members are African American and Hispanic. City College of San Francisco has Hispanic, Asian, and African American board members. At Maricopa in Arizona, half the board is women.

Hill-Collins would explain that the cultural heritage of representatives makes a difference when boards are confronted with community issues, because trustees are members of the same community (Hill-Collins, 2010). They know its history, experiences, students, businesses, and economic conditions. They have the social capital that is "grounded in a more just and equitable society" (Valadez & Rhodes, 1996, p. 25). Such perspective imprints a consciousness that resists the superior–inferior dualism prevalent in the ideas of a "common" culture or the tenets of acculturation. Trustees who envision critical multiculturalism as a basis for governance understand that urban institutions have unique characteristics derived from both the environment and character of their cities.

Sociologists Berger and Luckmann (1966) changed the paradigm of scholarly analysis with their emphasis on the social construction of reality. Their work led others to focus on the imbalance between those who own the discourse of language and research and those who, due to the oppression of their voices, have never made contributions to knowledge. As a community college practitioner and researcher, I have the unique opportunity to write contemporaneously and explore, to give voice to the silent and suggest direction for the future. I begin by summarizing the analyses of governing boards presented by contemporary research. Then, based on experience as a university research professor and community college faculty member, president, board member, and chair, my focus will turn to the challenges facing trustees as they seek to engage current issues and those yet to be identified.

Current Knowledge

Scholarly research on college trustees focuses primarily on six basic themes:

- A language that refers to them (governance, government, corporate structure)
- A focus on the ideas of governance and its meanings (shared governance; union, faculty and student governance; decision making; external and internal governance)
- A distinct reference to organizations acting as governance umbrellas (the Association of Community College Trustees, or ACCT; the Association of Governing Boards of Universities and Colleges, or AGB; the American Association of Community Colleges, or AACC; and the American Association of University Professors, or AAUP), and concepts that discuss their structure (collegial, professional bureaucracy, academic bureaucracy, organized anarchy, political system)
- A plethora of references to their contemporary challenges (lack of knowledge, incentive, and time; the question of whether boards govern or manage; relationships with the president, faculty, students, community, and other governmental agencies; appointed versus elected; and inner divisiveness)
- Generalized description of their roles and responsibilities (effectiveness of boards; crises in the college; policy and fiduciary responsibilities; facilities development and management; assessment, accountability, and evaluation of themselves and college president)
- A characterization of their "types" (rogue; representative of the public good; renegade; ethical leader; change agent; fundraiser; good/poor communicator; advocate for the college; keeper of institutional image; politically savvy; and split, divisive, and lay boards).

Notably absent from that long list is any reference to values, which are a critical part of board decisions. How can an urban college effectively deal with as much as 90% of its student population needing remedial education? How does it handle all the dire, socioeconomic implications of poverty?

What should it do to address failing K–12 school systems that produce precious few high school graduates ready for college-level work?

After decades of steady and sometimes soaring growth, enrollments in secondary and postsecondary schools have leveled off or been declining since the 2007–2008 economic crisis in the United States. The *Los Angeles Times* recently reported that enrollment in California's community colleges had "plunged to a 20 year low"—declining 21% between 2008 and 2012 (Rivera, 2013). With the largest community college system in the nation, California declined overall from 2.9 million to 2.4 million students in 2007–2012. From the perspective of Baltimore City Community College, which lost 21% of its enrollment in 2012, this means less state money and fewer resources; for an urban college with 60% of students living in poverty, it also means they are much less able to pay the higher tuition that usually results from state budget cuts.

So how do boards prioritize their values when confronting huge monetary losses? If they are focused on student success, good grades, and course completion, trustees must question how they make up for the loss of revenues by looking to the college–community relationship. Without increasing tuition, BCCC's budget shortfall is being reversed by an accountability plan based on the values of agency and collaboration. The process has included program assessment, reduction of staff through natural attrition (retirement and resignation) and new incoming grants, especially in the STEM fields (science, technology, engineering, and math) so important to the economy of tomorrow.

Emphasis on Community *and* Education

Boards are entrusted with the stewardship of their institutions; they exhort others to understand the importance of higher education by encouraging a responsible citizenry, better quality of life and career preparedness. These noble values are often at odds with the challenges of poverty, insufficient housing, inadequate health care, poor high school achievement, educational gaps in learning, and unhelpful public transit. The realities can seem insurmountable to trustees who deeply value and care for their communities. How do they offer appropriate sites for the various pockets of populations within the city? Where will the money come from? What should be the relationship between the board and its urban neighbors—city schools, businesses, and churches–and who defines it?

The American Association of *Community* Colleges (AACC) grew up from AACJC (the *J* was for *Junior*) in 1992, when members voted to change the title in part to convey the true scope of their universal mission. In the late 1990s, influential practitioners such as James Gollattscheck, Ervin Harlacher, and Patrica Cross advocated for educational programming *and* community services. This new dual emphasis directly increased enrollment, developed collaborative economic growth and clarified the value of community colleges in the improvement of the urban quality of life (Gollattscheck & Harlacher, 1997).

Local boards determine how to best provide academic programming as well as other noncredit and social services tailored to their specific constituencies. A growing number of food pantries on urban campuses, for example, provide students and others with groceries and sometimes clothing. There are usually little to no additional costs associated with such services, which can greatly amplify the college's impact on the community. Noncredit instruction, such as accounting, computer technology, and auto mechanics, is an effective way to recruit beginning learners into more advanced credit courses. Customized training programs in partnership with local businesses may result in a certificate of employability initially, followed by a related associate degree and university transfer later. Trustees who know their neighborhoods better than anyone pay special attention in such ways to help promote a productive and contributing citizenry, which in turn creates familiarity, respect, and support for the institution itself.

Governance Guides Actions

It has been said that "current community college governance suffers from poor design and poor execution" (Davis, 2000, p. 1). Many others would concur. Umbrella organizations such as the AACC and AGB offer considerable training and conferences to help trustees do a better job of public service. Many urban boards deserve to be criticized for their deficiencies. Perhaps, however, their training deserves special emphasis on the distinctive issues of city blight and the adverse repercussions they can have. Without such consciousness, we "create educational structures that prepare students from lower socioeconomic classes for nonprofessional careers without stressing their potential to assume leadership positions in social, political, and economic institutions, (and) a representation of class is made" (Valadez & Rhodes, 1996, pp. 23–24).

As put by well-known author, speaker, and Princeton professor Cornel West, one must come to terms with previous struggles to create more honest and empowering self-representations. Urban boards are similarly charged to commit themselves to more genuine self-representations as they define their particular governance models. They are also well-advised to comprehend the politics and power centers around them, because the college's performance will surely be scrutinized and judged by those same forces in return.

Politics and Power

Political influence is usually seen as a power maneuver. Both appointed and elected boards are involved in policy and political relationships. Board policies reflect student, faculty, staff, and community needs, all competing

NEW DIRECTIONS FOR COMMUNITY COLLEGES • DOI: 10.1002/cc

simultaneously. Legislatures want to hold colleges and their trustees accountable for high costs and low graduation rates. Political relationships occur not just at the national, state, city, and local levels, but among board members, too. More than anyone else, trustees must respond to all by meeting the expectations of oversight agencies as well as their own institutions and constituencies. Their relationship with the college president is critical in all issues, but takes on special significance at the political and policy levels. Very strong presidents and less powerful board members are an uneven match, usually resulting in less favorable college policies and performance. According to research by Vaughn and Weisman (1998), the longer presidents serve, the more they rely on personal and sometimes poor judgment. Problems including misallocation of funds, physical violence, and commission of felonies have been recorded. Too often, power can be a corrupting force; that's why we have trustees and presidents alike—to keep each other in check while working together for the public good.

How boards relate to external politics is reflected in their evaluations— governors and county commissioners tend not to reappoint dysfunctional members, and voters often choose not to reelect them. The media can make mincemeat of such colleges and their unresponsive or ineffective trustees.

In most studies of leadership, power, and politics are central to performance and solving problems. The uniqueness of urban colleges and their boards demands accountability as well as a collective voice of advocacy. In my own experience as both a college president and board member, I have reflected on the differences in each of those roles and the powers attributed to them. Presidents are judged by their individuality—one voice for the many. Boards are judged by their single voice—from many as one. For both, training and experience aid the presentation of voice; consciousness must precede the potential for abuses and misuse of power. For the urban board with such heavy responsibilities, the caveat *do no harm* must be incorporated into their code of ethics and behavior. Otherwise, failure to uphold the interests of students and community can jeopardize the college's affordability, accessibility, and relevance.

Conclusion: Be True to Mission and Values

Questions raised here are just a few that urban boards confront daily. Bylaws dictate how many times to meet a year, while literature explains the importance of relationships with the president. These concepts, however, are secondary to the reality of missions, values, opportunities, communities, politics, and power. Reflect on the emphasis that made the people's colleges unique among higher education in America. They emerged from within to better the average citizenry and locale. Part of their yet-untold story is the need to understand the optimum place of the urban college and board in governance and policymaking.

NEW DIRECTIONS FOR COMMUNITY COLLEGES • DOI: 10.1002/cc

Thoughts of the urban college bring to mind the poet Emma Lazarus' famous phrase, inscribed on our Statue of Liberty: "Give me your tired, your poor, your huddled masses . . ." she wrote, whereas we say give us the underserved, the undereducated, and the underemployed.

Ten Recommendations for Future Governance

1. Ensure the mission–vision is integrated into the fabric of the institution. In an urban setting, this usually means the broadest possible scope of board–community–business relations.
2. Explain and affirm institutional values around the urban mission, its foci in the community and among students. In some urban institutions, as many as 90% of students are urban poor and in need of developmental (remedial) coursework that is critical to their lifelong success and therefore should be a cornerstone of the college mission.
3. Ensure that the board is the outreach arm of the president of the institution. Urban colleges in particular must have a face and identity throughout the often-distrustful or unfamiliar community. Boards must monitor and evaluate the effectiveness of the college and the college president among all constituencies.
4. Audit and study the business of the board—budgets, real estate, hiring, everything.
5. Maintain the macro view of the college internally and externally to all constituencies. Compare to benchmarks at other similar institutions.
6. Manage change for the institution. In an urban setting, this process does not happen overnight. The job of the board is to maintain a macro view of the college and its environment.
7. Keep diversity as a board identity—involve state, regional, and local interest groups. Urban representativeness is essential.
8. Use research as an underpinning for board involvement and action, as advised by legendary management consultant Peter Drucker (2001). And always strive to celebrate, console, and produce as recommended by educational psychologists Lee Bolman and Terry Deal (2011).
9. Understand the politics of colleges, boards, and elected officials.
10. Maintain a thorough and continuing evaluation of board protocol, which may well include an ongoing assessment of the effectiveness of boards.

References

Berger, P. L., & Luckmann, T. (1966). *The social construction of reality: A treatise on the sociology of knowledge.* New York, NY: Random House.
Bolman, L. G., & Deal, T. E. (2011). *Leading with soul: An uncommon journey of spirit.* San Francisco, CA: Jossey-Bass.

Davis, G. (2000). *Issues in community college governance: Charting the second century of community colleges* (Report Number 7). Annapolis, MD: The Community College Press, American Association of Community Colleges.

Drucker, P. (2001). *The essential Drucker: The best of 60 years of Peter Drucker's essential writings on management.* New York, NY: Harper Collins.

Gollattscheck, J. F., & Harlacher, E. L. (1997). *Community building colleges lead the way to community college revitalization.* Washington DC: The Community College Press, American Association of Community Colleges.

Hill-Collins, P. (2010). The new politics of community. *American Sociological Review*, 75(1), 1–30.

Polonio, N. (2011, Fall). Case study: Preparing for change on the board. *Trustee Quarterly: The Voice of Community College Leaders.* Washington, DC: The Association of Community College Trustees.

Rivera, C. (2013). Community college enrollment at 20-year low. *Los Angeles Times* (March 26). Retrieved from http://articles.latimes.com/2013/mar/26/local/la-me-0326-college-cuts-20130326

Valadez, J. R., & Rhodes, R. A. (1996). *Democracy, multiculturalism, and the community college: A critical perspective.* New York, NY: Taylor and Francis.

Vaughn, G. B., & Weisman, I. A. (1998). *The community college presidency at the millennium.* Washington, DC: The Community College Press, American Association of Community Colleges.

ROSEMARY GILLETT-KARAM *is an associate professor of higher education at Morgan State University and director of its community college leadership doctoral program. She also chairs the board of trustees at Baltimore City Community College. Prior to arriving at Morgan in 2002, she was the president for five years of Louisburg College in North Carolina.*

NEW DIRECTIONS FOR COMMUNITY COLLEGES • DOI: 10.1002/cc

In the first chapter of this sourcebook, one of the scenarios presented for the future urban community college was that of a "workforce development college." In this scenario, the college of the future is the primary provider of a highly educated and talented community workforce in alignment with regional employment and economic development needs. A second scenario was that of a "social equity college" serving as a primary leader, advocate, and implementer of community-wide efforts to shape a multiracial democracy. The chapter concludes by stating that the best future will be created by linking the two scenarios, expanded upon here by exploring ways to close employability and wealth gaps.

The Employability Gap and the Community College Role in Workforce Development

Gunder Myran, Curtis L. Ivery

Black unemployment is double the national average. Whites in America have 20 times the median household wealth of black households and 18 times that of Hispanics, and the gap is only increasing. Racial and ethnic minorities are expected to comprise a significantly larger proportion of future workers, yet tend to be less prepared for the jobs of tomorrow. Students from this population are also more likely to attend a community college. However, only a small percentage complete a certificate or associate degree program leading to a good job and career advancement. It is therefore vital from educational, economic, and equity perspectives that urban community colleges play a leadership role in closing the employability and wealth gaps.

The United States has a long way to go before eliminating racial and ethnic disparities in degree production and strengthening the domestic workforce to remain internationally competitive. As put by Anthony Carnevale, director of the Georgetown University Center on Education and the Workforce: "The inescapable reality is that ours is a society based on work. Those who are not equipped with the knowledge and skills to get,

New Directions for Community Colleges, no. 162, Summer 2013 © 2013 Wiley Periodicals, Inc.
Published online in Wiley Online Library (wileyonlinelibrary.com) • DOI: 10.1002/cc.20058

and keep, good jobs are denied the genuine social inclusion that is the real test of citizenship. Those denied the education required for good jobs tend to drop out of the mainstream culture, polity, and economy" (Carnevale, 2012, p. 26).

It has been said that the first step to human liberation is a good job. It empowers individuals to grow in all areas of their lives, including support of family, cultural and recreational activities, continuing education, and career advancement. Many constituencies of the urban community college are struggling to get that first good job, or to recover from an economic reversal, and thus to gain a foothold on economic security for themselves and their families. These include African American males, immigrants and other non-English speaking persons, single parents, displaced workers, veterans, and other racial/ethnic minorities.

For them, urban community colleges offer a welcoming hand similar to that of settlement houses in the past. Starting in the late 1800s, settlement houses in bigger cities helped immigrants assimilate into American society and make the transition to the labor force. During the mass migration of African Americans from the South to northern industrial centers, black churches created such places to help migrants with employment, education, and social services. They also became havens from racial prejudice and advocates for public policies to combat poverty (Harvard, n.d.). Contemporary urban community colleges serve the similar purpose of empowering diverse groups to assimilate into American society and make the transition to employment and career advancement. They also address the structural inequities that create barriers to success for racial and other minorities and exacerbate the growing income and wealth disparities in our nation.

Definitions of Career Education and Workforce Development

Sometimes called vocational, occupational, or career and technical education, *career education* is generally regarded as associate degrees, certificate programs, and individual courses that prepare students for entry-level employment and career advancement. *Workforce development* has traditionally referred to noncredit job-skills training for individuals and customized employee training for a specific business or industry delivered in a continuing education format. However, workforce development is also emerging as a more inclusive term encompassing all the strategic initiatives of the college designed to contribute to the shaping of a highly educated and talented workforce in support of regional economic recovery and growth. In this sense, it includes economic and social equity initiatives, college and career readiness programs, dual enrollment in cooperation with school districts, and the building of corporate and community partnerships. To assure that a holistic view is articulated, it is now common to refer to *career education and workforce development* initiatives.

The Community College Middle-Skill Careers Niche

A generation ago, the typical American had a reasonable outlook for attaining middle-class status as a result of talent, ambition, and hard work. Today it is essential to add two components to achieve a middle-class lifestyle: lifelong education and social equity. The 2006 Spellings Commission Report for the U.S. Department of Education estimated that 90% of the fastest-growing jobs in the new knowledge-driven economy will require some postsecondary education in the form of an associate degree, certificate, or license (Spellings, 2006, p.1). The Center on Education and the Workforce at Georgetown University reports that 21% of all jobs fall into this sub-baccalaureate or middle-skill career level (Carnevale & Smith, 2012, p. 22). The center defines middle-skill careers as those producing annual earnings of $35,000 or more, although some generate in excess of $75,000 In fact, there is substantial overlap between the highest-income middle-skill careers and the lowest-income careers requiring bachelor's degrees. For example, a computer programmer with an associate degree may earn twice as much as an early childhood educator or social worker with a bachelor's degree.

Middle-skill careers that require an associate degree have typically been offered in employment areas such as accounting, automotive services, computer information systems, law enforcement, emergency medical technology, nursing, pharmacy technology, dental hygiene, surgical technology, hospitality management, fire protection, and culinary arts. And, in fact, the majority of new nurses and other health care workers do receive their education at community colleges, as do up to 80% of first responders such as fire protection workers, police officers, and emergency medical technicians. In recent years, in response to technological advances and changing employment patterns, community colleges have introduced associate degrees in areas such as biotechnology, cyber investigation and computer forensics, environmental technology, geothermal systems technology, video game design, and web design and development.

Another development is the dramatic expansion of certificate programs, usually up to one year in length. These are modularized and stackable programs tailored for the unique workforce needs of a specific community or industry. Certificate programs lead to careers in areas such as aircraft dispatching, baking, dietary management, energy technology, facility management, industrial maintenance technology, medical billing and coding, real estate sales associate, medical imaging, quality control technology, and unmanned aerial systems.

The Equity Imperative

A major challenge faced by urban community colleges is to design effective responses to the mismatch between career opportunities offered by regional labor markets and the capacity of residents to take advantage of them. For example, Detroit is the fourth-most segregated large city in the nation after Milwaukee, New York, and Chicago (PSC, 2010). Residents of inner-city Detroit have the highest unemployment rate and live the furthest distance from available jobs of any other major city in the nation. Population has declined by 61%, or more than 1 million residents, since 1950. Public schools are under state-appointed emergency financial management. The high school dropout rate is nearly twice the state average, and half of the mostly black adults are functionally illiterate. In July 2013 the former seat of America's industrial might became the biggest city in U.S. history to file for bankruptcy.

In what Cornel West has called "pathology of despair" (Ivery & Bassett, 2011, p. xii) in such urban environments, the Wayne County Community College District is a singular beacon of hope and a primary advocate for shaping a multiracial democracy in the Detroit metro region. WCCCD is at the fore of efforts to overcome the persistent and entrenched racial, educational, economic and social inequities threatening the city, the region, and by extension the state and nation.

In 2002, WCCCD partnered with other community organizations to sponsor a national educational summit in Detroit, *Responding to the Crisis of Urban America*. The summit addressed dimensions of the urban crisis, such as illiteracy, unemployment, concentrated poverty, residential segregation, and mass incarceration of African American males. The goals were to create social awareness and identify practical solutions that could be implemented across America. For its part, WCCCD launched in 2002 the *Pathways to the Future* initiative to transform the district's programs, services, facilities, structures, and systems in response to the urgent and often unmet career and other educational needs of the citizens of Wayne County including Detroit.

Since 2002, thanks to increased millage support from local voters, WCCCD has transformed its career education and workforce development programs. District-wide enrollment has increased dramatically to more than 70,000 credit and noncredit students. A number of new associate degree and certificate programs in career education have been added, and the district's engagement with community partners to have a positive impact on the economic, educational, social, and cultural dimensions of community life has expanded substantially. WCCCD is now positioned for enduring excellence through a focus on student success and college-wide effectiveness.

The Emerging Themes of Career Education and Workforce Development

In recent years, urban community colleges have launched a number of innovations in career education designed to create a closer match with the changing knowledge and skill requirements of the workplace. These include school-to-college pipeline initiatives, summer bridge programs, work-based and experiential learning, dual enrollment, learning communities, imbedding of student support services into career education programs, corporate colleges, microloan projects, business incubators, stackable courses and programs, and encore career programs for older displaced workers. The framework below outlines the major themes of these emerging continuing education and workforce development initiatives:

Program Innovations

- *Student Completion Agenda:* Upgrade programs, services, and institutional systems to increase the number and percentage of students who complete a college-level certificate program or an associate degree, or transfer to a baccalaureate-level college or university.
- *College and Career Readiness:* Upgrade student orientation, advising, first-year college experience, and other programs that address career and academic planning, study skills, time and financial management, and transition to the collegiate environment.
- *Environmental Scanning:* Use "big data" or analytics approaches to identify changing workplace knowledge and skill requirements as a basis for program innovation.
- *Pace of Career Education and Workforce Development Programming:* Speed up the pace of program innovation, increase investment in program development, and strengthen faculty professional development activities.
- *Merging of Credit and Noncredit Instruction:* Break down the boundaries between credit and noncredit (continuing education) programming and between career education and liberal arts education; shift the focus of program development on the identified job skills and career advancement requirements of targeted student or community groups.
- *Contextualized and Accelerated Developmental Education:* Link the development of basic literacy skills to learning that relates to the career objectives of students; imbed the learning of basic literacy skills into the objectives and teaching of career education courses. Accelerate the pace at which students develop basic literacy skills through summer bridge programs and other intensive instructional designs.
- *Education-to-Employment Pipeline:* Create a clear and seamless pipeline encompassing transition from high school to community college and from community college to baccalaureate institution.
- *Experiential or Work-Based Learning:* Incorporate on-the-job learning into all career education programs through approaches such as work-study, internships, and simulation.
- *Structured Career Pathways:* Transform the pathways students take to their career objectives through easily accessible on-ramps, a more proscribed curricular structure, fewer and less confusing program choices, and incentives to complete a college credential.

Strategic Innovations

- *Changes in College Policies:* Consider policy changes that increase the potential for college and career success, such as required admissions testing and course placement.
- *Dual Enrollment:* Partner with K–12 school districts to offer college-level courses and programs to high school students who qualify; sponsor charter schools with a focus on careers in high-demand occupations.
- *Economic and Social Equity:* Address individual, institutional and societal inequities that allocate opportunities and support in ways that unfairly disadvantage racial and other minorities in terms of participation in career advancement and the economic mainstream.
- *Corporate and Community Partnerships:* Address ways business, educational, governmental, nonprofit, and religious leaders can cooperate to create a world-class workforce as a dimension of regional economic development strategies; increase involvement of employers in driving program innovation at the school and college levels.
- *Community Educational Leadership:* Lead the integration of the economic and workforce development initiatives of all educational institutions in the community or region to holistically create a highly skilled and talented workforce in the region, including K–12 schools; other community colleges; baccalaureate institutions; governmental units; nonprofit agencies; organizations offering basic adult education, ESL, and GED programs; churches; and other community groups having an educational mission.
- *Local, State, and National Governmental Policies:* Participate in addressing infrastructure issues (housing, employment services, transportation, justice, etc.) that limit economic and workforce development and create inequities in job and career opportunities.
- *Career-Oriented Student Support Services:* Imbed student support services such as career and academic advising, peer tutoring, financial aid support, and personal counseling directly into career education programs.
- *Faculty "Community of Peers":* Empower career education faculty members to create dialogue opportunities for the exchange of teaching and learning ideas and practices.
- *Accountability for Student Learning Outcomes:* Strengthen processes for assessing student learning outcomes and ensuring institutional accountability for "moving the needle" in terms of achieving program outcomes that match the changing demands of the workplace.

General Education for Knowledge Workers

One of the distinguishing characteristics of the community college compared to for-profit business colleges is that all community college students take general education or liberal arts courses as a degree completion requirement. All students, whether in career or academic programs, share courses in disciplines such as English, humanities, social sciences, natural sciences, and mathematics. Because all programs share the common experience of general education, these courses become the "glue" that gives the curriculum cohesion and wholeness. For career education students, this experience is an opportunity to transcend their career field to develop knowledge and skills in areas needed in the knowledge economy, such as critical thinking, problem solving, communication, and teamwork. As well, the community college seeks to develop in all students the well-rounded attributes that bind us as a nation and give life meaning and richness, such as respect for diverse cultures, interpersonal skills, aesthetic appreciation, creativity, and civic responsibility.

Toward Solutions: Career Education and Workforce Development Practices

Urban community colleges across the country are redesigning their career education and workforce development programs to meet the dual objectives of employability and equity. Below are examples of how some are activating the innovative themes outlined above:

- St. Louis Community College is leading a consortium of nine Missouri community colleges in creating the Missouri Manufacturing Workforce Innovation Network. Funded by a U.S. Department of Labor Trade Adjustment Assistance Community College and Career Training grant, the program provides opportunities for displaced workers and under-skilled adults to prepare for careers in advanced manufacturing.
- The Baltimore City Community College (Maryland) Year Up program provides opportunities for low-income young adults to learn career-related skills through classroom-based learning, hands-on skill development, and a paid internship at a Fortune 500 company. The first cohort graduated in 2013 and completed internships with companies such as John Hopkins Hospital and Health System, Morgan Stanley, T. Rowe Price, and Domino Brands. Year Up is a nonprofit organization devoted to closing the "opportunity divide" for urban young adults who possess immense talent but all too often are stranded outside the economic mainstream.
- Chattanooga State Community College (Tennessee) has created the Focused Learning System, which centers on the alignment of desired institutional-level learning outcomes with those at the course, program, and discipline levels. This system starts by involving employers and CSCC faculty and staff in determining the institutional-level outcomes expected of certificate and degree completers. Faculty and staff are then

mandated to develop student-learning outcomes aligned to these institutional outcomes. Finally, student performance data from all levels is integrated to provide a basis for mapping student progress and determining if the system is producing an increasing number of completers in an efficient manner.

- Guilford Technical Community College (North Carolina) has championed the success of high school students who are historically "lost" in the education pipeline between high school and college (J. Roueche & Roueche, 2012, p. 68). GTCC has embraced the primary–16 pipeline concept by providing a number of specific programs that create a seamless system of education from K–12 to the community college level. These include middle colleges, early colleges, college tech-prep program, and the Guilford Area School Assistance Program (advising and marketing program for high school students who are undecided about college-going plans).

- The Community College of Philadelphia (Pennsylvania) sponsors the Center for Male Engagement, a program to empower men from diverse backgrounds to attain a college degree and pursue a career. One dimension is summer enrichment for African American males enrolling in college for the first time. The summer program includes sessions on academic success, communications, financial literacy, leadership development, masculinity, race and academic success, and time management.

- The Louisiana Community and Technical College System offers a *Day One Guarantee* to students. If an employer finds that a graduate is deficient in one or more competencies, the college will retrain the employee at no cost to the graduate or employer. This program reinforces LCTCS's commitment to involving businesses in developing curricular standards and assuring business-validated specifications for each career education program.

- The City Colleges of Chicago operates veterans' services centers at each of its colleges. Staffed by teams that include military veterans, the centers address the unique challenges returning veterans face when making the transition from active duty to college life. The centers provide one-on-one services as well as a welcoming environment where veterans can meet, network, relax, or study.

- Presidents play a central leadership role at the national level as advocates for full minority access to the economic mainstream and American dream. They are active on national boards and commissions of organizations devoted to addressing the career and educational needs of underprepared and underserved groups. These national organizations include the American Association of Community College's Commission on the Future of Community Colleges, Achieving the Dream, Jobs of the Future, Learn to Earn, Completion by Design, Gear Up, Breaking Through, and Year Up.

NEW DIRECTIONS FOR COMMUNITY COLLEGES • DOI: 10.1002/cc

Summary: Middle-Skill Talent Drives Economic Growth

Talent trumps all other factors in the economic recovery and growth of urban centers. In support of the regional economy, urban community colleges are becoming the primary source of middle-skill talent through their career education and workforce development programs. According to the Lumina Foundation, by 2018 two-thirds of all jobs in the nation will require at least a college-level certificate, associate degree, or licensure (Lumina, 2012, p. 5). Thus, community colleges will be a central driving force on the "education to employment highway."

References

Carnevale, A. (2012). Preparing America for middle-skill work. *Community College Journal, December 2012/January 2013*.

Carnevale, A., & Smith, N. (2012). Skills match: Colleges equip students with the tools to land important middle-skill career. *Community College Journal, December 2012/January 2013*.

Harvard University Open Collections Program (n.d.). Settlement house movement. *Immigration to the United States, 1789–1930*. Retrieved from http://ocp.hul.harvard.edu/immigration/settlement.html

Lumina Foundation (2012). *A stronger nation through higher education. How and why Americans must achieve a big goal for college attainment*. Retrieved from www.luminafoundation.org/publications/A_stronger_nation.pdf

Ivery, C. L., & Bassett, J. A. (Eds.) (2011). *America's urban crisis and the advent of color-blind politics: Education, incarceration, segregation, and the future of U.S. multiracial democracy*. Lanham, MD: Rowman & Littlefield.

Population Studies Center (PSC), Institute for Social Research, University of Michigan (2010). *Race segregation for largest metro areas (population over 500,000)*. Retrieved from www.psc.isr.umich.edu/dis/census/segregation2010.html

Roueche, J. E., & Roueche, S. D. (Eds.) (2012). *Rising to the challenge: Lessons learned from Guilford Technical Community College*. Washington, DC: Community College Press, American Association of Community Colleges.

Spellings (2006). *A test of leadership: Charting the future of U.S. higher education*. A report of the commission appointed by Secretary of Education Margaret Spellings. Retrieved from www2.ed.gov/about/bdscomm/list/hiedfuture/reports/final-report.pdf

GUNDER MYRAN *is president emeritus of Washtenaw Community College in Ann Arbor, Michigan. Prior to his 23-year tenure as WCC's president, he served as a professor in administration and higher education in the College of Education at Michigan State University. He is also a faculty member and national advisory board member of the Doctorate in Community College Leadership at Ferris State University.*

CURTIS L. IVERY *has been chancellor of Wayne County Community College District in Detroit since 1995. For his work at WCCCD and numerous writings, including publication of America's Urban Crisis and the Advent of Color-Blind Politics in 2011, he has become a nationally recognized authority on urban affairs.*

6

This chapter explores the evolving landscape of the urban college from the perspective of Cuyahoga Community College in Cleveland. It frames innovative and creative ways to develop unique partnerships with local high schools and employers, exemplified by the best collaborative practices of Cuyahoga and other community colleges.

Reframing Community Partnerships

Jerry Sue Thornton

Community colleges are reinventing themselves to meet the evolving needs of all constituent groups including students, businesses, and local social interests. Given the even faster pace of change occurring in urban environments, colleges serving this sector are experiencing disproportionate pressure to transform.

Metropolitan areas are highly influenced by racial, social, cultural, age, religious, and economic factors in a rapidly changing environment. The 2010 U.S. Census found that 84% of Americans live in a metropolitan area. Compared to 2000, the U.S. population is larger, older, and more diverse, with rapid growth in some areas of the country and sizable population declines in others.

Of the 27.3 million population growth between 2000 and 2010, 25.2 million occurred in metropolitan areas. Growth varied by regional size; areas with 2000 populations of 2.5 million to 5 million grew the fastest, as did those in the south and west. The fastest declines were in two areas in Louisiana and Arkansas, and three areas in Ohio, Pennsylvania, and West Virginia.

As an indicator of changing race and Hispanic-origin distribution, every metro area in the country had a smaller non-Hispanic white share of the population in 2010 compared to 2000. In the most recent U.S. census, nearly two-thirds of the population was non-Hispanic white, one-sixth was of Hispanic origin, and the black population accounted for one-eighth. Non-Hispanic whites declined as a share of the whole in every statistical area, while the Hispanic population increased between 2 and 4 percentage points over 10 years in all areas.

New Directions for Community Colleges, no. 162, Summer 2013 © 2013 Wiley Periodicals, Inc.
Published online in Wiley Online Library (wileyonlinelibrary.com) • DOI: 10.1002/cc.20059

In 2010, the median age of the U.S. population was 37.2 years, up from 35.3 in 2000. Metropolitan populations were younger (36.6), with higher percentages in four youngest age groups up to 44. The 25–34 age group is located much more often within cities than suburbs. Embedded in those statistics are the risk factors that affect many of the populations in urban and metropolitan areas struggling to improve their economic status through education. While urban universities enroll some students with risk factors, a disproportionate number are registered in community colleges, where they fail more often than classmates without such deficits.

Identification of significant risk factors has been researched and written about over the years in the following ways: The first step includes a review of the literature to determine the risk factors and conditions that increase the likelihood of students dropping out of school/college, and the second step is to analyze how these risk factors have an impact on behavior. Based on Hammond, Linton, Smink, and Drew (2007), 25 significant risk factors across eight categories are most meaningful in urban areas. Approximately 60% of the factors are individual-related, and the rest are attributable to family.

Individual risk factors include learning disability or emotional disturbance; early adult responsibilities such as work and parenthood; social attitudes, values and behavior; and school performance, engagement, and behavior. Family background risk factors include low socioeconomic status, high mobility, low education level of parents, large number of siblings, absence of natural parents, and family disruption. Lack of family commitment to education also contributes to risk factors of low educational expectations, sibling dropouts, and slight contact with school.

The two risk factors most common among dropouts are independence from family and part-time attendance. The latter is especially relevant to the 65% of community college students who take classes less than full-time.

Environmental Risk Factors Compel Combined Response

The American Association of Community Colleges (AACC) acknowledges that "compared with students at four-year public and private institutions, community college students are much more likely to come from low-income households, to be the first-generation college students, and to attend part time while working or taking care of children" (AACC, 2012, pp. 13–14). While risk factors have a particularly negative effect on urban students, the real risk is to the American dream and the potential for each succeeding generation to climb out of poverty.

In a powerful book, R. Roosevelt Thomas, Jr. (Thomas, Gray, & Woodruff, 1992) makes an eloquent case for understanding the environmental factors that influence success or impede progress, and making the appropriate changes in attitudes and behavior to achieve different outcomes. Thus, achievement at community colleges in metropolitan areas depends on a shared vision of possibilities as proposed by Roueche, Baker, George, & Rose (1989), who advocate transformational leadership in American community colleges.

The challenges for urban community colleges seeking greater academic success for more students are so daunting that it requires all engaged entities to fully combine their expertise and resources for the common good. Forging a shared vision for collaboration between community and college is critical for all, and best attained through partnerships.

The authors of *Shared Vision* assert that through a mutual decision-making process, community needs and college goals are addressed in a way that promotes openness and an understanding of the importance of change (Roueche et al., 1989). Partnerships establish the equality of participants utilizing the assets each brings, resulting in the greatest potential for successful outcomes. If a partner lacks equity in the relationship, the results will be tainted. Having a shared vision with comparable capital enhances the likelihood of joint ownership of the results or achievements.

Partnerships with the best chance of success are based on equity and mutual respect. Imperative if urban colleges want to work closely with community entities, Drucker (1999) espouses a *genuine* partnership based on respect, trust, predictability, and balance. These characteristics comprise the very foundation on which urban life rebounds. Without these qualities, emerging collaborations will lack longevity.

Thus, partnerships with urban community colleges require groups to join forces toward a common vision for the common good. It also calls for mutual respect and clear understanding of roles. Any imbalance in the relationship creates dissonance that requires adjustment of contrasting obligations, structure, processes, ways of interacting, communications and other areas of collaboration.

Many excellent examples of community college partnerships are indicative of the benefits of collaboration. Community colleges across the country internationally realize that tackling the enormous issues of urban life cannot be approached singularly. Urban colleges need collaborative relationships with an emphasis on development of students, community, and business.

Selected Best Partnership Practices

Cuyahoga Community College's Early College High School.   Cuyahoga Community College, in partnership with the Cleveland Metropolitan School District, created the Design Lab Early College High School, which opened in 2008. It is one of more than 240 such schools opened or redesigned since 2002 around the country in conjunction with the Early College High School Initiative. The schools enable 75,000 low-income, first-generation college goers, English language learners, students of color, and other young people underrepresented in higher education to simultaneously earn a high school diploma and an associate's degree or up to two years of credit toward a bachelor's degree tuition-free.

Cleveland's is a new and innovative, design-themed STEM (science, technology, engineering, and mathematics) school where students are thinkers, problem solvers, and learners taking a variety of classes that focus on art and industrial design. The hands-on curriculum features a rich mix of activities to foster a career path from high school to college and beyond.

The vision for the new high school is to teach important skills that change students from just telling us what they know to using what they know to demonstrate what they can create. Its culture is one in which failure is but a prelude to success. It is truly learning by doing and delivering of education. The school does not accept the notion that high school is practice for future jobs; rather, in this age of Google and instant access to information, the future is *now* for students who attend the Design Lab. They engage in practical learning activities much like their future jobs.

The primary goal of the partnership was to create a clear and coherent program beginning in ninth grade to give every student the opportunity to earn college credit while attending high school. Often referred to as dual enrollment, it provides many pathways to an associate's degree. Most importantly, Design Lab seeks to ensure that graduates will not need remediation to prepare for college-level courses. The Early College High School Student Information System reports a graduation rate of 84% at 250 high schools in 2010, compared to 76% in their local districts. Nearly 80% of graduates went on to some form of postsecondary education (Early College Designs, n.d.).

A new school culture in this case makes both teachers and students feel appreciated and comfortable taking risks, measurable by attendance and referral data, the number of suspensions, and student surveys. In addition to creating an environment of care, respect, and rapport, learning goals focus on shifting instruction to the application of learning outcomes. The school moves students from traditional high school expectations to those of higher learning and, in some cases, honors. Faculty have an opportunity to gain training in the College Board Advanced Placement so they can support student advancement by raising the rigor of high school courses and promoting success.

With a 2013 enrollment of 220 students, the regional public high school offers an excellent opportunity to collaborate with top faculty in the Cleveland public schools and Cuyahoga Community College, as well as access to world-class facilities in which to study and implement design principles. Students work with the college engineering program, which offers foundational coursework in industrial design, media arts, and other related programs.

Skills taught in the Design Lab prepare young people for the careers of today and tomorrow, and cultivate a highly skilled workforce for corpora-

NEW DIRECTIONS FOR COMMUNITY COLLEGES • DOI: 10.1002/cc

tions within the region. Northeast Ohio has thousands of unfilled jobs in the STEM industries due to a lack of skilled workers. The Design Lab curriculum was developed with input from the greater Cleveland business community to ensure the area schools are educating students to meet the workforce needs of regional companies.

Sinclair Community College: A New Model of Collaboration. Sinclair Community College in Dayton, Ohio, has a long history of partnerships with Dayton Public Schools. One is the $36 million career technology high school that opened in 2009 adjacent to the college campus. The school serves 750 students (grades 9–12) with a unique curriculum of 16 career programs in five pathways jointly developed by the college and high school faculty. The college invested $4 million by purchasing technical lab equipment, equipping and operating a college-prep tutoring center, and offering college scholarships. This investment results in a deep partnership and connectivity for students, and allows the college to use the high school facilities for courses during off-hours.

College enrollment results are remarkable. In 2012, 61% of the high school's graduates enrolled at Sinclair. This is by far the highest percentage of any school graduating class from a region of more than 100 high schools. For comparison, the average enrollment from the 16 high schools (as a group) nearest Sinclair is 22% of graduating students. Additionally, of the 250 juniors and seniors at the high school, about 200 attend Sinclair and receive college credit while in high school.

St. Louis Community College: A Value Partner to Aerospace Industry.   St. Louis Community College has a long legacy of serving the needs of the aerospace industry. For more than 20 years, the college has partnered with aerospace and aviation companies large and small to deliver cutting-edge workforce programs.

Despite losses in manufacturing jobs over the past decade, St. Louis is home to 31 aerospace and manufacturing firms, including the headquarters for Boeing's Defense, Space, and Security unit, DRS Sustainment Systems, GKN Aerospace, and many smaller suppliers employing more than 14,000 workers. Aircraft assembly workers are projected to grow by 8.6% over the next decade with significant job vacancies due to retirement.

Boeing fuels much of this demand. In recent years, the company expressed serious concerns about the lack of skilled assembly technicians to replace large numbers of Baby Boomers nearing retirement. With assistance from the State of Missouri Division of Workforce Development, St. Louis Community College's Workforce Solutions Group, and the Emerson Center for Engineering and Manufacturing on STLCC's Florissant Valley campus, a joint venture with Boeing was formed. The focus is to develop and implement a pre-employment training program as an ongoing pool of candidates for employment with Boeing.

The award-winning program was designed and developed by staff from Boeing and STLCC based on curriculum provided by Boeing, including hands-on demonstration projects. Each session provides 408 hours of instruction over 10 weeks in aircraft assembly techniques, accessing computer-based work instructions, and teamwork. There is no charge to students, as training costs are covered by Boeing, the college, and state.

Twenty-three sessions have been completed since November 2007, with 206 students completing training and 175 employed at Boeing and GKN Aerospace for an 85% job placement rate. The program was recently cited as a model to grow the community college system in India by Tara Sonenshine, the undersecretary for public diplomacy and public affairs for India's Ministry of Human Resource Development (STLCC, 2013).

In partnership with Boeing, GKN Aerospace, and small aerospace companies, STLCC has leveraged the success of this program into an Aerospace Institute through a U.S. Department of Labor Community-Based Job Training grant. The Institute offers courses in aerospace fundamentals, blueprint reading, metal structures, electrical and mechanical assembly, and installation, and composites fabrication and assembly.

The institute has now added a partnership with Gateway STEM High School in St. Louis. STLCC is working with local aviation companies to develop an FAA-certified Airframe and Power Plant Maintenance (A&P) program. The program will provide an affordable pathway for high school students to graduate with their licenses. There is also the opportunity for an adult-learner pathway. Both populations are expected to be active in the employment pool for not only Boeing, but many other aviation companies in the greater St. Louis area. These A&P programs ensure that the college will continue to build on its legacy as the premier provider of aerospace and aviation training in the St. Louis region.

Summary

Bob Davis and David Wessel write that the pathway to the middle class is through education, and that much of the education for the masses will happen in community colleges. They view education as improving human productivity, then spreading the added wealth throughout society. Community colleges are referred to in the book and by practitioners at large as the *people's colleges* for their open-door policy. Urban community colleges truly belong to and are of the people that they serve, and are pathways to a better quality of life. They are, however, only able to achieve success in this great endeavor with help and support from many corners of their communities.

By uniting with public schools, business, industry, and other civic and community organizations, these uniquely American inventions capitalize on the resources around them to make all more effective in the process. They look for opportunities to help employers grow and prosper, doing the same in return for their students by training them to meet the exacting requirements of high-paying, high-tech areas like the aerospace industry. And even in the immediate absence of such industries to partner with, they enhance the future consideration of their communities by collaborating with public schools in areas like high-demand STEM programming to advance the economic viability of populations who could not otherwise realize the American dream.

References

American Association of Community Colleges (AACC) (2012, April). *Reclaiming the American dream: Community colleges and the nation's future, a report from the 21-century commission on the future of community colleges.* Retrieved from www.aacc.nche.edu /aboutcc/21stcenturyreport/21stCenturyReport.pdf

Davis, B., & Wessel, D. (1998). *Prosperity: The coming twenty-year boom and what it means to you.* Crown Business.

Drucker, P. F. (1999). *Management challenges from the 21st century.* New York, NY: Harper Collins.

Early College Designs (n.d.). *Jobs for the future: Overview and FAQ.* Retrieved from www .earlycolleges.org/overview.html#outcomes1

Hammond, C., Linton, D., Smink, J., & Drew, S. (2007). Dropout risk factors and exemplary programs. Clemson, SC: National Dropout Prevention Center and Communities In Schools, Inc.

Roueche, J., Baker, G., George, A., & Rose, R. (1989, April). *Shared vision: Transformational leadership in American community colleges.* Washington, DC: The Community College Press, American Association of Community and Junior Colleges.

Thomas Jr., R., Gray, T. I., & Woodruff, M. (1992). *Differences do make a difference.* Atlanta, GA: The American Institute for Managing Diversity, Inc.

St. Louis Community College (STLCC) (2013, February 11). STLCC-Boeing partnership noted at international conference. *STLCC Now* (website). Retrieved from http:// now.stlcc.edu/?p=1558

JERRY SUE THORNTON retired in June as president of Cuyahoga Community College in Cleveland, the largest community college in Ohio. During her tenure since 1992, "Tri-C" grew from 23,000 to 32,000 students and added two corporate colleges, a campus in Westlake, and a center in Brunswick. Prior to that, she served for seven years as president of Lakewood Community College in White Bear Lake, Minnesota.

As one of the country's biggest and most diverse institutions of higher education, Miami Dade College (MDC) has also grown into a leader among urban community colleges operating in very similar conditions. Here, MDC President Eduardo J. Padrón summarizes the extra measures behind a graduation rate that is among the highest for this sector of the most underprepared postsecondary students.

Increasing the Relevance of Curricular and Student Services in the Urban Community College

Eduardo J. Padrón

In 1960, the sway of history brought a shockwave of transformation to South Florida. The revolution in Cuba, just 90 miles south of Key West, sent a tide of 50,000 immigrants across the Florida Straits. South Florida and Miami became the country's vanguard of demographic and cultural transformation. At the time, non-Hispanic whites represented nearly 80% of Miami-Dade County (then Dade County)'s population. Ten years later it was 45% Hispanic, 33% non-Hispanic white, and 23% black. This sunlit vacation spot had a new and rapidly developing ambiance.

Like America itself, Miami Dade College's evolution as an institution of multiracial democracy started out in reality as quite the opposite. Dade County Junior College opened for classes in fall 1960 with two mostly segregated campuses, one for 1,200 white students at the Central Campus and the other for 185 blacks at Northwestern. Seven of the more qualified blacks were permitted to take classes at Central in that first semester, followed by 10 in spring 1961. During the next academic year, 1961–1962, no sophomore classes were offered at Northwestern because few initial enrollees made it through their freshman year. That fall, 72 black sophomores enrolled at Central and 258 at Northwestern, 163 of whom also took one or more classes at Central. Northwestern ceased to exist the following year, making DCJC (now Miami Dade College, MDC) the first integrated junior college in Florida and the first integrated public college in the old Confederacy (Cohen, 1964).

New Directions for Community Colleges, no. 162, Summer 2013 © 2013 Wiley Periodicals, Inc.
Published online in Wiley Online Library (wileyonlinelibrary.com) • DOI: 10.1002/cc.20060

The initial separation of blacks and whites reflected the persistence of segregation in Florida's public schools, despite being ruled unconstitutional nationwide in 1954 by the U.S. Supreme Court decision Brown v. Board of Education. Today, however, MDC serves as a model of multiracial democracy—defined as "a goal for a nation founded on the principle of human equality" (Ivery & Bassett, 2011, p. 133)—with one of the highest graduation rates in the country for its urban sector and a student population that is 87% ethnic or racial minorities.

By 1962, 1,500 to 2,000 Cuban immigrants were arriving in Miami each week, and the college's population grew to 6,000. Despite the inclusion of more than 200 blacks, its new multiethnic makeup was dominated by burgeoning white and Hispanic enrollment. Dade Junior College was cited that same year by the Greater Miami Urban League for "taking firm progressive steps."

By 1964, enrollment had swelled to 13,000. Operation Pedro Pan brought 14,000 children ages 6–17, most of whom joined the public school system before arriving at the open door of Dade Junior. By 1967, it was the largest institution of higher education in the state, with 23,341 students. It was the fastest growing junior college in the nation, enrolling more freshmen than the University of Florida, Florida State University, and University of South Florida *combined*. It had also become one of the nation's most diverse, and like all the other big-city community colleges, a haven of learning opportunities for people seeking a fresh start or better life.

Miami and its community college have continued the trend ever since. Cubans and other residents of Latin American origin make up nearly 65% of the county's population. Others from the Caribbean and around the globe contribute to one of the planet's richest urban tapestries. Central to educational and economic growth, MDC has maintained its open-door policy and now welcomes students speaking 94 languages from 185 countries. With 99,000 credit and noncredit students across eight campuses, it is one of the nation's largest public institutions of higher education.

Evolution of an Academic Institution

MDC in the 1960s and early 1970s was very much a reflection of the times. Academic programs offered alternatives to the coursework and standards of Florida's state universities. It welcomed everyone, particularly those who could not get into more traditional and selective institutions. Programs were characterized by a wide range of choices and the freedom to invent independent study. Courses were delivered via TV long before the Internet. In addition to traditional arts and sciences majors, a number of occupational programs began to appear, including aviation, police and fire science training, and allied health.

Early data on student success showed that a more structured and rigorous general education foundation was required. Between 1975 and 1978,

NEW DIRECTIONS FOR COMMUNITY COLLEGES • DOI: 10.1002/cc

MDC questioned whether open access could be successfully combined with excellence and high standards. It tightened admission standards but still maintained an open door to those with a high school diploma. The institution established a set of general education requirements for all students, who were additionally expected to adhere to new standards of academic progress (SOAP). While standards were decidedly elevated, so too was the college's commitment to a new level of academic support. But with the introduction of SOAP, another tacit tradition of the early years fell away: Many students who had shown little progress were asked to leave.

These reforms represented a defining moment for MDC and many other colleges watching with interest. They signified a response to new urban and demographic challenges by melding the equally important priorities of access and academic excellence.

Expanding Opportunities in an Urban Context

The institution continued to address the shifting cultural and ethnic base of the community. Bilingual studies became a full-fledged division in 1979, with more than 2,000 students enrolled at the InterAmerican Center in Miami's Little Havana neighborhood. It was soon to become the largest bilingual learning facility in higher education—just in time for the 1980 Mariel boatlift that brought an additional 125,000 Cuban refugees to the United States, most choosing Miami as their new home. The college responded by addressing Cuban as well as an increasing number of Haitian immigrants with its Haitian/Hispanic Employability through Language Program (HELP).

In the ensuing years, MDC has continued to add programs that reflect the needs of a maturing regional economy and ethnically diverse community. The college has expanded to eight campuses and numerous outreach centers across Miami-Dade County. In addition, MDC's Virtual College enrolls more than 12,000 students annually, larger than the student population of three MDC campuses.

Several academic advances continue to reflect the college's awareness of the economic and personal challenges of a primarily low-income urban community. In 2002, MDC launched its honors college, an accelerated, full-time, two-year program that prepares exceptional high school graduates for continued study at many of the finest universities in the country.

The introduction of bachelor's degrees in 2001 provided low-income students with an additional avenue to advancing their prospects for meaningful and well-paid employment. The first bachelor's degrees, offering teacher preparation in secondary math, several science majors, and exceptional education, returns many graduates to teach in the schools and neighborhoods from which they came. In addition, 16 more baccalaureate degrees were offered, including nursing; supervision and management; electronics engineering; information systems technology; biology with emphasis in biotechnology and biopharmaceuticals; film, TV and digital technology; and early childhood development. Partnerships with the world of work are very extensive, as industry advisory teams collaborate with MDC's 12 professional schools regarding curriculum and job placement.

The college has also championed the arts as a vehicle for learning and understanding, available to both students and the broader community. At little or no cost to the community, MDC hosts one of the nation's most heralded literary events, the Miami Book Fair International, as well as the Miami International Film Festival and art galleries at each campus. Fine arts degrees in visual and performing arts are offered at all campuses.

In 1984, MDC added an arts conservatory, New World School of the Arts, which awards high school through baccalaureate degrees in partnership with Miami-Dade County Public Schools and the University of Florida. An additional high school, School for Advanced Studies (SAS), is available at four MDC campuses. In the past two years, both New World and SAS have been ranked by *Newsweek* (America's best high schools, 2012) and *U.S. News & World Report* (Best high schools, 2013) among the best high schools in the nation.

Learning Outcomes: Defining a College Education

Throughout its history, MDC has reinforced the foundations of liberal education. Traditional arts and sciences programs have shared the curriculum agenda with occupational tracks responsive to workforce trends. But in 2006, MDC put that foundation under a 21st century microscope trained on the dramatic changes affecting society and higher education. In an era of new knowledge and challenges, the project set out to clearly define what it meant to gain a Miami Dade College education.

Ownership by faculty, staff, and students is critical, as are two additional values repeated constantly: *Intentionality* of our efforts and *authenticity* of learning. *Intentionality* suggests that everything we do—in the classroom, service learning, and student life—has an obvious and identified connection to one or more of the learning outcomes. Faculty syllabi, for example, began to connect topics and assignments to particular outcomes. *Authenticity* compels us to penetrate beneath the prevailing completion criteria; it implies a depth of understanding and the ability to apply learning to current, real-life situations. The very ambitious ultimate goal was transformation that could shift the course of student lives.

The project continues to be driven by faculty, with strong support not only from student services personnel but also from the Greater Miami Chamber of Commerce and several industry leaders.

Ten Liberal-Learning Outcomes

Identifying learning outcomes implies the redefinition of liberal education. The Liberal Education and America's Promise (LEAP) initiative by the

Association of American Colleges and Universities (AAC&U) offers a broad context that emphasizes the lasting tradition of "empowered individuals with the knowledge and skills to address complexity, diversity and change" (AAC&U, n.d.). But making that tradition relevant demands awareness of the shifting landscape of science, culture, and society. At MDC, faculty honed a wide range of options to 10 liberal-learning outcomes expected of graduates:

- Communicate effectively using listening, speaking, reading, and writing skills.
- Use quantitative analytical skills to evaluate and process numerical data.
- Solve problems using critical and creative thinking and scientific reasoning.
- Formulate strategies to locate, evaluate, and apply information.
- Demonstrate knowledge of diverse cultures, including global and historical perspectives.
- Create strategies that can be used to fulfill personal, civic, and social responsibilities.
- Demonstrate knowledge of ethical thinking and its application to issues in society.
- Use computer and emerging technologies effectively.
- Demonstrate an appreciation for aesthetics and creative activities.
- Describe how natural systems function and recognize the impact of humans on the environment.

The learning outcomes reflected the AAC&U-commissioned survey by Peter D. Hart Research Associates (2006, 2010) that produced the term "360-degree people." Business leaders said they wanted specific skills relevant to given fields, and yes, they wanted technological acumen too. But more importantly, they wanted people who could think critically, solve problems, and work effectively as team members. And more—they wanted people who were conscious of cultural diversity and trends in sustainability that might benefit their enterprises. In essence, they were defining a new, well-rounded, 360-degree world citizen.

MDC's learning outcomes include essential science, technology, engineering, and math (STEM) learning but do not minimize the importance of the humanities and social sciences, a trend all too prevalent today. Civic engagement and knowledge of the workings of a democratic society in the 21st century are also key elements. And the arts, too often relegated to discretionary status, are regarded as essential for learning.

Mapping Curriculum

The learning-outcomes mapping project ensures that graduates have sufficient opportunity to achieve all 10 objectives reflected throughout each degree program. This required the review of more than 2,000 courses. A

NEW DIRECTIONS FOR COMMUNITY COLLEGES • DOI: 10.1002/cc

mapping template allowed faculty to record the level of learning outcomes covered—emerging, developing, or proficient. Also recorded was a pre-scription to introduce, reinforce, or emphasize various outcomes. This pro-vides an avenue to enrich particular courses with deeper engagement of learning outcomes. Lastly, faculty documented co-curricular support, which might include service learning in a range of community contexts or campus life activity. No set number of outcomes is to be covered in each course, but students should have repeated practice in all the outcomes by the end of their program experience.

When the mapping project was complete, each program and depart-ment had produced a comprehensive spreadsheet that detailed the state of learning outcomes. The project continues as an ongoing cycle of college-wide review to strengthen student performance.

Assessing the Culture of Evidence

At MDC we had spoken for years of the need to develop a culture of evi-dence driven by data and informed understanding. If authenticity is a cen-tral value, intuition and anecdote alone are insufficient indicators of desired results. The work of assessment involves several fronts. An essential need is to evaluate student understanding of the learning outcomes in the aggre-gate. In this sense, we produced a snapshot of achievement allowing for comparisons from year to year and necessary adjustments to curriculum, teaching methods, and assessments.

Our particular assessments are in the form of real-life scenarios provid-ing students the opportunity to demonstrate the level of their mastery. In most cases, the scenario tasks offer the chance to address several of the learning outcomes. For example, one scenario asks the student to review information about oil extraction in the local environment and respond to several prompts about a proposal to drill in Biscayne Bay. Another asks for response to several prompts about the creativity, beauty, and cultural per-spective of a work from architecture or the arts.

Learning outcomes are measured against a scoring rubric that identi-fies four thoroughly articulated levels of mastery. Faculty take assessment very seriously. It remains a creative and rigorous process that continues to grow in each specific discipline.

The State of American Education: Challenges Persist

Given the cutbacks in state education funding across the nation over the past 30 years, it should surprise no one that the international Organisation for Economic Development and Cooperation (OEDC) ranked U.S. 15-year olds 17th in reading, 23rd in science, and 30th in math among advanced nations in 2010. OEDC's Programme for International Student Assessment (PISA) also stated that all but four of the 65 participating nations "place at

NEW DIRECTIONS FOR COMMUNITY COLLEGES • DOI: 10.1002/cc

least an equal, if not a larger, number of teachers into socio-economically disadvantaged schools as they do in advantaged schools" (OEDC, 2010, p. 9). The United States was among the four exceptions, meaning our socioeconomically disadvantaged schools also tend to be exceptionally deprived of basic resources. Unlike ours, most other countries' urban students performed better on the test than those from outlying areas. For a nation with 82% of its population regarded as urban, the disparity is significant.

The College Board (2012) found that only 43% of students taking the Scholastic Aptitude Test (SAT) achieved the college/career-ready benchmark, indicating the likelihood of higher grades and retention. For students whose parents' education did not include a bachelor's degree, the SAT benchmark was achieved by only 27%. All of the preceding data suggests that in multicultural, urban, low-income America, the price for neglect is severe and generational, as evidenced by the pronounced era of remediation in which we now find ourselves.

Turning Challenges into Successes

The above challenges are certainly present in our corner of the education landscape. Seventy-two percent of Miami Dade College students arrive underprepared in at least one basic skill area; 46% are living in poverty and 67% are low-income. The overwhelming majority work while taking classes, and 56% are the first member of their family to attend college. Despite these outsized challenges, MDC's three-year graduation rate of 25% nearly doubles that of comparable large urban community colleges, based on 2011 data from the National Center for Education Statistics' Integrated Postsecondary Data System.

Credit is due to a corps of faculty members who embrace teaching and continue to learn via an active college-wide training and development initiative. Many are adept with classroom technology and social media that address varied learning styles and connection with students. A strong college-wide engagement with service learning also ensures a practical component. But MDC's success is built primarily on a broader commitment to produce a surrounding environment for students from the first moments of their college experience.

Despite our success, 25% is only 25%—and still below the average 28% graduation rate for all 978 public community colleges in 2011. The challenges remain formidable, as we all lose far too many students whose success or failure affects communities across the country.

Student Achievement Initiatives

MDC's Student Achievement Initiatives (SAI) aims to further improve every phase of academic, social, and financial processes to make them as efficient as possible in the interest of degree and certificate completion

NEW DIRECTIONS FOR COMMUNITY COLLEGES • DOI: 10.1002/cc

while maintaining access and quality. The project originated as one of three partnership grants from the Bill and Melinda Gates Foundation's Completion by Design, a five-year program that works with community colleges to significantly increase completion and graduation rates for low-income students under 26. Along with the two other cadres in North Carolina and Ohio, we are aiming to produce national models for student success. Additional support from the Lumina, Kresge, and Knight Foundations, among others, have added components to the project. We have researched and planned, and now begun to implement much of our understanding.

Our planning seeks to improve the student experience according to how ready or not they might be for college. One of the most glaring points in our research is that those who complete at least half their required course credits and 25% in their major area in their first year are twice as likely to finish their degree. Clearly, we need to find ways to reinvent developmental education, shorten its duration, and help students to identify a major area of study and remain consistent to it over time. All of this and more need to be accomplished by close attention to learning outcomes. The following aspects of SAI are beginning to make an impact on the short-term solutions that yield the greatest initial impact—early outreach to incoming students:

Test Preparation Before Starting Classes.   During the summer of 2012, all incoming fall students received emails stressing the importance of placement testing. Intensive instruction in reading, writing, and math—a developmental "boot camp" of sorts—has enabled half of the students who tested into the higher levels of college prep to improve at least one developmental level.

Noncognitive Diagnostic Assessments.   MDC piloted the ENGAGE instrument developed by ACT to measure the motivation, self-regulation, and social engagement of 7,500 students, because noncognitive factors are relevant in supporting those who are new to the rigors of higher education. Results are discussed with advisors and appropriate supports are identified.

Mandatory Orientations for All Incoming Students.   In 2012, the college mandated in-person, new-student orientations with student services and financial aid staff on all eight campuses. They become familiar with important campus resources, initiate academic advising, and complete on-site registration for classes. Orientations encourage students to be accountable for learning and, in consultation with an advisor, to clarify an academic path that meets their aspirations and program needs.

Intensive First-Semester Academic and Career Advising.   The notion of intrusive advisement is a key factor in the MDC Student Achievement Initiatives. Choosing courses that align with program and degree requirements, as well as transfer to other four-year institutions, is imperative. As a mandate, advisors support students in the development of an individual education plan that facilitates effective decisions regarding educational, transfer, and career goals. Advisors also refer students to additional internal and external resources and support services.

Improving Pathways from High School to College. College readiness is a crucial factor that requires close working relations between different administrations, faculty, and staff. MDC admits more than 69% of graduates from the nation's fourth-largest public school system who attend public colleges or universities in Florida. The college has established a geographical feeder pattern with the county's high schools and works regularly with school administrators and advisors. Summer bridge and other college preparatory initiatives have been in place for many years.

Hispanic Access to College Education Resources project (¡HACER!, Spanish for "to do") is a new development in SAI. It is a collaborative initiative with the Lumina Foundation and 17 community partners, including Univision, the City of Miami, Greater Miami Chamber of Commerce, Miami-Dade County Public Schools, Bank of America, and Florida International University, to support access and success for Latino high school students. Activities include professional development for high school counselors on college readiness, content-based English for academic purposes for language learners, and extensive exploration with the Chamber of Commerce regarding internships, mentoring, and scholarships.

Sustained Improvements in Student Experience

SAI is a multi-year initiative that addresses MDC's historic foundation of academic excellence and student support. The longer-term activities include the following:

Academic Redesign. This is difficult but creative work that will provide more structured curriculum plans with sequential coursework at all levels. This effort will focus on the top five disciplines—business, biology, criminal justice, psychology, and health sciences—that represent 80% of MDC students, as well as developmental and LEAP on-ramps.

Better Integration of Academic and Support Services

- *Coaching and Mentoring.* MDC is developing a more intrusive structure to support these academic programs. Students will continue to receive coaching and mentoring each semester, either in person or through online modules, via a partnership of student services and faculty advisors. The college is also developing an online dashboard technology that will allow advisors to track student progress and address the most pressing needs.
- *Student Success Experience.* MDC is also developing a model for comprehensive orientation and success courses, career readiness skills, and career-related experiences for students at multiple levels in their college career.

- *Communities of Interest.* This is a key element in providing a reasonably sized and reliable support environment. Communities of interest will align curriculum, services, faculty, staff, and physical/virtual spaces with students' career interests.
- *Integrated Learning Support.* Technology must play a key role in an institution of MDC's size. The challenge is to define a model that integrates high tech with the necessary high touch, and uses all resources appropriately.

Conclusion: Sharing the Universal Resource of Higher Education

Like everyone else, Miami Dade College is asking questions that reflect the anxiety of a new era. We want to know what it will take to be secure and successful in the future. What will constitute an educated person? What will become of our democratic traditions in these changing times?

Community colleges are the nation's best hope for addressing issues of a globalized knowledge economy. They are the solution to stagnant economic and social mobility, the rising costs of four-year institutions, and powerful demographic changes that demand an open door to higher education for the bulk of America's low-income urban residents.

College success is no longer optional. Studies by the U.S. Department of Education, the Georgetown Center on Education and the Workforce and others clarify that the overwhelming majority of jobs being created in the United States require postsecondary education. Prosperous communities and a competitive nation rely on increasing numbers of low-income students gaining the skills to successfully navigate a new economy.

Evidence-Driven Change Works Best.   MDC's efforts suggest a number of cornerstone tenets in providing students a supportive environment. Developmental support is a reality that must be embraced with relevant measures. In the same spirit, "It takes a village" is a necessary attitude regarding reforms that require ownership by faculty and staff.

Steps should be based on reliable evidence of what works and does not. For MDC, it has translated into hundreds of faculty and staff formulating new academic pathways and supportive elements; overall, a more comprehensive and integrated learning environment results. If we are to fulfill the critical role of nourishing a healthy urban democracy, we must evolve our systems from the worthy principle of access to the necessary standard of completion. Contained within that goal is a depth of learning and transformation that defines our institutions and students.

References

American Association of Colleges and Universities (AAC&U) (n.d.). *What is a 21st century liberal education?* Retrieved from www.aacu.org/leap/what_is_liberal _education.cfm

America's best high schools 2012 (2012, May 26). *Newsweek*. Retrieved from www .thedailybeast.com/newsweek/2012/05/20/america-s-best-high-schools.html

Best high schools 2013 (2013). *U.S. News & World Report*. Retrieved from www.usnews. com/education/best-high-schools

Cohen, A. M. (1964). *Miami-Dade Junior College: A study in racial integration* (Unpublished dissertation). Florida State University, Tallahassee, FL.

Peter D. Hart Research Associates (2006). *How should colleges prepare students to succeed in today's global economy?* (Report conducted on behalf of the Association of American Colleges and Universities). Retrieved from www.aacu.org/leap/documents/ Re8097abcombined.pdf

Peter D. Hart Research Associates (2010). *Raising the bar: Employers' views on college learning in the wake of the economic downturn* (Report conducted on behalf of the Association of American Colleges and Universities). Retrieved from www.aacu.org/ leap/documents/2009_EmployerSurvey.pdf

Ivery, C. L., & Bassett, J. A. (Eds.) (2011). *America's urban crisis and the advent of color-blind politics: Education, incarceration, segregation, and the future of U.S. multiracial democracy*. Lanham, MD: Rowman & Littlefield.

Organisation for Economic Co-operation and Development (OECD) (2010). *Programme for International Student Assessment (PISA) 2009 results: Executive summary*. Retrieved from http://www.oecd.org/pisa/pisaproducts/46619703.pdf

The College Board (2012). *SAT® Report: Only 43 Percent of 2012 College-Bound Seniors Are College Ready*. Retrieved from http://press.collegeboard.org/sat

Related Resources

Miami Dade College (n.d.). *The 10 learning outcomes*. Retrieved from www.mdc.edu/ learningoutcomes

Carnevale, A. P., Smith, N., & Strohl, J. (2010). *Help wanted: Projections of jobs and education requirements through 2018*. Washington, DC: The Georgetown University Center on Education and the Workforce. Retrieved from http://www9.georgetown.edu/ grad/gppi/hpi/cew/pdfs/fullreport.pdf

Under construction: Twenty-five years of Miami-Dade Community College, 1960–1985 (1983). Tulsa, OK: Miami-Dade Community College in conjunction with Lion & Thorne, Ltd.

Cuban Refugee Center Records, 1960–1978 (n.d.). University of Miami Cuban Heritage Collection. Retrieved from http://proust.library.miami.edu/findingaids/?p=collections/ findingaid&id=46&q=&rootcontentid=5552#id5552 1500.html

EDUARDO J. PADRÓN has been president of Miami Dade College since 1995. He arrived in the United States at the age of 15 as a Cuban refugee in the same wave of immigration from that revolution-torn country described in this chapter. His first higher education experience was as a student at MDC, which he has since been credited for transforming into an institution of both national and global prominence.

NEW DIRECTIONS FOR COMMUNITY COLLEGES • DOI: 10.1002/cc

8

The goal of multiracial equity is not just a phrase in mission statements, but a top-down strategic necessity for community colleges founded on and dedicated to the principles of social justice. At a system like Maricopa with more than 200,000 diverse credit and noncredit students at ten colleges—including six classified as urban—in the greater Phoenix area, it takes the entire institutional community to achieve such a goal.

Achieving a Multiracial Democracy on Campus

Rufus Glasper

As community colleges, "democracy's colleges" and the open door to educational opportunity for millions of postsecondary students, the concept of multiracial democracy is foundational to our mission. This chapter conceptualizes multiracial democracy through the lens of social justice, and more specifically Rawl's eloquent argument for equality of opportunity, which makes it incumbent on us to rethink market-driven behaviors and petitions us to think first of those we often think of last. "[In] order to treat all persons equally, to provide genuine equality of opportunity, society must give more attention to those with fewer native assets and to those born into the less favorable social positions" (Rawls, 1999, as cited in Levin, 2007, p. 46). This is the social contract and civic obligation to which community colleges must hold themselves accountable.

Community colleges have "historically claimed the moral high ground for educating underserved populations—including those populations who are on the economic periphery of society ..." For them, the college "bears a particular responsibility for remedying unjust conditions for disadvantaged populations," argues Levin (2007, p. 185). As chancellor of the Maricopa Community Colleges, I know that the challenges are unrelenting. The work is demanding, requiring passion, commitment, resources and accountability. But it is the work that we do, the work that we must do.

Community colleges are the point of entry to postsecondary education for significant percentages of the nation's minority students. In 2012, 49%

New Directions for Community Colleges, no. 162, Summer 2013 © 2013 Wiley Periodicals, Inc.
Published online in Wiley Online Library (wileyonlinelibrary.com) • DOI: 10.1002/cc.20061

of African American, 56% of Hispanic, and 42% of Native American undergraduate students were enrolled in community colleges (AACC, 2013). We owe them more than a chance; we owe them a fair and equal opportunity to be successful on our campuses.

While community colleges historically have represented access and opportunity to the country's underrepresented minority students, there is inherent danger in the current course of declining resources, decreased access, and dismal completion and success rates. Community colleges are heavily engaged in initiatives to increase national degree and certificate completion by an additional 5 million students by the year 2020. These students will be nearing the 50/50 demographic mark, with recent reports noting that "by the year 2020, minority students will account for 45% of the nation's public high-school graduates" (Hoover, 2013). Hence, we must make multiracial democracy more than an educational axiom; it must be a priority in our social contract and a reality for our students.

"Diversity" is no longer just an initiative at the Maricopa Community Colleges; it is embedded into our culture. Once a predictable part of community college mission statements (Ayers, 2002) to share ethnic or cultural traditions, it has become a strategic and increasingly embedded, functional reality at our institutions, starting at orientation with its own strategic planning processes and related accountability for solid outcomes. Consistent with significant change in bureaucratic institutions, the process of weaving diversity into the organizational culture has been deliberate and iterative. This chapter describes a number of our successes and challenges, and conveys our ongoing commitment to social justice through equal educational opportunity for all students.

Diversity and equity encompass value statements that we foster throughout our organizational culture and, through the teaching and learning processes, attempt to instill in students. Maricopa Community Colleges are in Maricopa County, the Greater Phoenix area of Arizona. The district encompasses 10 independently accredited colleges, two skill centers, and numerous campuses and sites serving more than 200,000 credit and noncredit students. Maricopa also manages three radio stations and a TV station. Our students are increasingly diverse, as they are around the country.

Fall 2012 demographics portray a Maricopa student population that is 55% white, 21% Hispanic, 8% African American, 4% Asian, 3% Native American, and 9% ethnicity undeclared. In 2003, whites represented 59% and Hispanics 18% of the total student population. Student characteristics are representative of larger demographic changes, as the Greater Phoenix area is one of the fastest-growing for the Latino population. Between 2001 and 2010, Arizona's Latino growth rate was 46% (Hart & Hager, 2012), and Latinos now constitute nearly a third of the state's population.

But for us, planning for Arizona's changing demographics began more than 20 years ago. As a district, equity is deeply ingrained in our culture—

part of the way we do business. It has taken commitment, innovation, and follow-through, but we are proud to share that in 2012 the Maricopa Community Colleges were the Association of Community College Trustees' national winners of the Charles Kennedy Equity Award.

This chapter shares our commitment and a sampling of initiatives specific to supporting multiracial democracy on our campuses. They are categorized within Myran's (2009) "common ground" for shaping an inclusive environment, creating the opportunity for everyone to achieve full potential, and recognizing our community colleges as living laboratories for diversity and social justice.

Creating the Opportunity for Everyone to Achieve Full Potential Starts at the Top

It is clichéd to suggest the importance of the phrase "It starts at the top," but as public community colleges, the significance of having consistent, well-defined leadership for initiatives as important as multicultural democracy is worth reviewing. As a multicampus district, we understand and appreciate that one of the most important roles of our governing board is leadership. Our board is charged with identifying outcomes for the purpose of better serving our constituencies, which include the people of Maricopa County, students, employers, universities, and K–12 institutions. It is for our communities that we work to provide not only specific academic opportunities, but the longer-term socioeconomic benefits that come as a result of our responsibility to provide for social justice. But it must start at the top. Our governing board is committed to the concept of multiracial democracy, and as a five-member, publicly elected body, is itself diverse.

As part of our social contract, the Maricopa Community College Board has developed a vision, mission, values, goals, guiding principles, and policies that demonstrate equity and the enhancement of opportunities for minorities and women. Examples of how the commitment starts at the top are evidenced by the language of our policy documents, some of which are shared below:

Maricopa Community Colleges' Vision Statement

A community of colleges—colleges for the community—working collectively and responsibly to meet the lifelong learning needs of our diverse students and communities.

Mission Statement

The Maricopa Community Colleges create and continuously improve affordable, accessible, effective, and safe learning environments for the lifelong educational needs of the diverse communities we serve.

Institutional Values

The Maricopa Community Colleges are committed to:

- *Community:* We value all people—our students, our employees, their families, and the communities in which they live and work. We value our global community of which we are an integral part.
- *Honesty and Integrity:* We value academic and personal honesty and integrity and believe these elements are essential in our learning environment. We strive to treat each other with respect, civility, and fairness.
- *Inclusiveness:* We value inclusiveness and respect for one another.

Maricopa Community Colleges' Guiding Principles

Respect: Embrace and support diversity. Treat all people with dignity. Listen actively to various opinions. Encourage and support the development of all to meet their potential.

Governing Board Statement on Diversity

The Maricopa Community Colleges support a diverse and inclusive environment where mutual respect and equity are encouraged and valued; one that actively seeks to understand and incorporate views from dissimilar frames of reference.
(Maricopa Community Colleges, 2013)

The Chancellor's Diversity Initiative

In developing an institutional culture, it is important to have not only principles and values, but a structural component that gives connection to the programs as well. The Maricopa Chancellor's Diversity Initiative is the overarching structure for diversity and inclusiveness efforts. An advisory council and its individual coordinators interface with other areas of the organization to provide information, consultation, research, and reports that promote diversity and inclusiveness in support of student success.

As chancellor, I consistently work from the platform of my diversity initiative. It includes affirmative action (i.e., leveling the playing field in recruitment and hiring), valuing diversity (appreciating individual differences and unique qualities), diversity management (creating and maintaining a positive environment where employee differences are recognized, understood, and valued), and inclusiveness (integrating individual differences and unique qualities of all people to transform how we do our work). These initiatives are integrated in the diversity strategic plan.

Diversity Strategic Plan

As noted, diversity is interwoven throughout our policy documents and planning frameworks. But it is not enough to espouse diversity and inclusion; we value what we measure, so we measure our progress related to diversity and inclusion. The Maricopa Community College Board requests ongoing evaluation of the district's diversity initiative. An annual diversity report presents the results of the strategic plan, which maps the components, directions, indicators, and projected outcomes of Maricopa's efforts to create an inclusive environment for all students and employees.

The Maricopa Diversity Advisory Council (DAC), composed of a large number of representatives from throughout the district, drives major initiatives. A persistent theme for DAC has been the importance of effective management of diversity as key to achieving the overarching goal of the organization. The council promotes a number of activities, programs, and services for students and employees. Each college and the district office have a designated diversity coordinator to assist in all efforts related to diversity and serve as DAC liaison.

The diversity strategic plan addresses the campus environment to create an inclusive organizational climate through a variety of initiatives including the chancellor's community advisory councils (small community groups representing various ethnic groups), as well as employee constituency groups representing the Association of Chicanos for Higher Education, Asian Pacific Islanders Association, Equality Maricopa (supporting lesbian, gay, bisexual, and transgender employees), Association of Chicanos in Higher Education, the Council on Black American Affairs, VOICE Maricopa (supporting employees with disabilities), and the Women's Leadership Group. These internal and external constituency groups provide additional perspectives on promoting and infusing diversity into the campus climate.

The inclusive climate is also promoted through training, grants, workshops, and seminars. One highlight is Maximizing Our Strengths as an Inclusive Community (MOSAIC), a 24-hour diversity/cultural competency workshop series for faculty and staff to increase awareness, develop skills, and create inclusive environments. More than 1,000 employees have participated in the program, which was recently adopted by student leadership as well. Students participated in for-credit communication classes about diversity, facilitation, cross-cultural communications, and small-group communication, then facilitated the program for their peers. The significance of student ownership given the social construct of multiracial democracy is noteworthy.

Recognizing Community Colleges as Living Laboratories for Diversity and Social Justice

Another facet of multiracial democracy is recognition that one size does not fit all in creating effective learning environments. This supports Myran's (2009) framework of colleges as "living laboratories" for social justice. All of our colleges provide numerous activities to support and educate students, faculty, staff, and community about our diverse populations.

NEW DIRECTIONS FOR COMMUNITY COLLEGES • DOI: 10.1002/cc

Exemplary efforts are recognized by the advisory council and shared with the larger Maricopa Community through the *Expressions Newsletter* to invite replication.

The diversity initiative creates an environment of inclusiveness that enables minority students to be successful. As suggested earlier, we value what we measure. Evidence of success includes improvements in completion rates for associate degrees in general studies over the past 10 years, nearly doubling for African American students and increasing slightly for Hispanics.

As we look to the future of college-wide inclusiveness we will continue to have student-learning outcomes and competencies attached to multicultural initiatives. The evaluation and assessment of learning outcomes is happening on campuses around the country, and we hypothesize that this will continue to gain momentum in the coming years as the initiative moves from being defined by activities and events to more mainstream learning outcomes. The following describe in more detail some of the opportunities, challenges, and successes of three programs in the living laboratories that are our campuses:

Hoop of Learning.   The Hoop of Learning is a high school bridge program that enables Native Americans to receive both high school and college credits. The goal is to provide the tools and initiative to increase academic achievement and provide a foundation for successful transition into college and other forms of higher education. Hoop of Learning has celebrated more than a decade of success and continues to grow.

Basic tenets of the model replicate the indigenous "Circle of Life" philosophy long practiced by Native American peoples of the North and South Americas. These tenets include lifelong development; developing strong positive cultural identities and integrity; culturally relevant education; traditional tribal community facilitated by a broad network of relations; individuals contributing to the well-being of the community; and Native people serving as role models.

The Maricopa Hoop of Learning aims to increase high school retention and graduation rates; increase Native American participation and matriculation rates into college; create conditions for retaining Native American students to reach their higher education goals; enhance culturally relevant curriculum; increase diversity on campuses; and strengthen external collaboration by establishing and continuing partnerships with Native American communities, school districts, and other agencies. Participants benefit from a scholarship supported by district and other tribal community funds that covers tuition, books, transportation, and meals. While earning college credit, Hoop of Learning students participate in cultural courses and workshops, take field trips, and provide volunteer service to their communities.

Minority Male Initiative.   The impetus for the Minority Male Initiative (MMI) in Maricopa was national statistics citing what was already apparent to many educators: Minority males were not achieving at the same academic levels as white males and minority females. This includes low high school graduation rates, low college enrollment rates, and poor retention and college completion rates. Nationally, just 28% of African American males ages 24–35 have at least an associate degree, compared to 70% of Asian, 44% of white, and 16% of Hispanic males (Lee & Ransom, 2011).

The MMI Committee was charged with reviewing similar programs across the country and harvesting best practices for use within Maricopa. Early meetings focused on areas for improvement including more targeted recruitment, more welcoming campus services, and enhancing the climate of the classroom. An early challenge was the need to not only create the program, but to initiate programs on each of the 10 individually accredited college campuses.

MMI uses a multifaceted approach that encourages academic achievement, promotes personal and professional development, and provides support for minority males to stay in college, graduate, and achieve their goals. Each spring MMI hosts an annual conference for students to network, expand their leadership skills, and learn about professional and academic resources. Students can interact with civic leaders, Phoenix business leaders, representatives from area universities and Maricopa County Community College District faculty, staff, and administration. Examples of conference sessions include leadership, academic success, and career preparation. A highlight is the mentoring session, where students directly interact with minority male professionals.

Each campus is also implementing a Male Empowerment Network (MEN) chapter for students to participate in both campus and district-wide team building, cultural and professional-growth opportunities. The development of MEN responds to one of the early planning challenges mentioned previously: the need to standardize support initiatives for minority male students at all 10 colleges versus having niche/boutique initiatives that would not have high-level presence, administrative support, or the appropriate structure to sustain the programs each year.

Achieving a College Education (ACE).   Another high-profile program, ACE is nationally recognized for its success in motivating underrepresented students to complete high school and continue on to finish a college degree. ACE was established in 1987 at Maricopa's South Mountain Community College in Phoenix, and has since expanded to each Maricopa campus. It now serves more than 17,000 students, 85% of whom graduate early or on time. The program helps make smooth transitions between three critical points of the educational pipeline: high school, community college, and university. Its success lies in nine essential elements:

1. *Creation of student cohort groups.* Students enter the program during the summer before their junior year of high school.

2. *Focus on at-risk students.* The program recruits students who fit at least one of the following criteria: first-generation college student; works 10–30 hours per week; from a single-parent home; from an under-represented group; experiencing environmental factors (foster care, teen parent, etc.); and sibling or relative of an ACE participant.
3. *High academic standards.* Students are concurrently enrolled in college courses while in high school. Faculty teach all ACE college courses; students must complete placement testing prior to enrollment and meet prerequisites for all courses.
4. *Non-threatening environment*
5. *Continuous contact with students*
6. *Family involvement*
7. *Strong collaboration between institutions*
8. *Long overlap of transition points* (e.g., high school to community college)
9. *Scholarship and financial aid information*

In addition to motivation to graduate from high school, ACE students are given the opportunity to earn up to 24 college credits while still in high school. For example, ACE students who graduated from high school between 1996 and 2010, and who were retained in the program, earned an average of 21 college credits before graduating from high school. The success of Maricopa's ACE program has led to development of other related initiatives. Jr. ACE is a bridge program that engages 5th- to 10th-grade students with experiences that enhance retention and create pathways to high school ACE and then on to postsecondary education. We have also created an ACE Native American Initiative, which has increased Native American student participation across all ACE programs by 30%.

As I look to the future of multiracial democracy and initiatives such as ACE, I see us continuing to widen the net of influence. We need to ensure that extended families share the benefits and challenges of higher education, and we need to influence the cultural capital among ethnic groups to ensure that postsecondary study is appropriately valued. An example is Adult ACE, a scholarship-based college- and career-preparation program for adults 16 and older. It offers students in adult basic education the opportunity to bring their skills up to college level in math and English while working toward their GED and provides a full range of support services to help them reach their goals.

Multiracial Democracy as Social Justice

I have argued that community colleges have a social responsibility for "advantaging the disadvantaged" (Levin, 2007, p. 185). It can only be accomplished by systemic, integrated planning and evaluation that start at the top and are encouraged and supported by initiatives cultivated in the living laboratories of our community colleges (Myran, 2009). The current economy favors individuals who have social and economic capital. Access to higher education elevates opportunities for social and economic mobility; successful completion is influenced by socioeconomic factors that we are responsible for mitigating through multiracial democratic initiatives, such as the few exemplified here.

Those programs for the most part have two sociocultural outcomes: They promote educational success for diverse students and begin to shift cultural norms to a framework of social entrepreneurism. The minority-male initiative empowers our young men to be leaders and change agents. ACE not only assists students with academic completion, but changes their families too. Systemic enculturation of such priorities requires persistent, thoughtful leadership by the institution and students alike. Making outcomes measurable creates tangible results critical to the democratic ideals we represent.

As I finalize this manuscript I'm looking at a picture of a row of policemen in Montgomery, Alabama, overseeing a march for black voting rights. We have come so far, but have so far to go. I am proud that our community colleges, despite increasing demands for scarce resources, have accepted our social responsibility for advantaging the disadvantaged. But "No, no, we are not satisfied, and we will not be satisfied until justice rolls down like waters, and righteousness like a mighty stream" (King, 1963).

References

AACC (American Association of Community Colleges) (2013). *Fast facts from our fact sheet*. AACC website. Retrieved from www.aacc.nche.edu/AboutCC/Pages/fastfactsfactsheet.aspx

Ayers, D. (2002, Winter). Mission priorities of community colleges in the southern United States. *Community College Review, 30*(3), 11–31.

Hart, B., & Hager, C. J. E. (2012). *Dropped? Latino education and Arizona's economic future*. Morrison Institute. Retrieved from http://morrisoninstitute.asu.edu/publications-reports/2012-dropped-latino-education-and-arizonas-economic-future/view

Hoover, E. (2013). Wave of diverse students will rise rapidly. *The Chronicle of Higher Education,* Jan. 10. Retrieved from http://chronicle.com/article/Wave-of-Diverse-College/136603/

King Jr., M. L. (1963, August 28). *I have a dream*. Retrieved from http://abcnews.go.com/Politics/martin-luther-kings-speech-dream-full-text/story?id=14358231

Lee, J. M. Jr., & Ransom, T. (2011, June). *The educational experience of young men of color; A review of research, pathways, and progress*. New York, NY: The College Board. Retrieved from http://advocacy.collegeboard.org/sites/default/files/EEYMC-ResearchReport_0.pdf

Levin, J. S. (2007). *Nontraditional students and community colleges: The conflict of justice and neoliberalism*. New York, NY: Palgrave.

Maricopa Community Colleges (2013). *Mission/Vision/Values, 2013*. Retrieved from www.maricopa.edu/publicstewardship/governance/boardpolicies/govprocess.php#values

Myran, G. (2009). Campuswide inclusiveness: Ensuring equity for diverse students. In G. Myran (Ed.), *Reinventing the open door: Transformational strategies for community colleges* (pp. 57–65). Washington, DC: Community College Press.

RUFUS GLASPER has been chancellor of Maricopa Community Colleges since 2003; he previously held leadership positions for more than two decades in the district. He is a member of numerous organizations committed to improving higher education on local, state, national, and international levels. He also serves on several community boards and has received numerous awards for his civic engagement and contributions to excellence in education.

NEW DIRECTIONS FOR COMMUNITY COLLEGES • DOI: 10.1002/cc

Urban community colleges face a myriad of convergent challenges, including the loss of state funding and local property tax support, increased demands for better performance and greater accountability, and record-high enrollment by the most underprepared students in higher education. Sometimes to make sense of it all, it helps to think of an onion.

Capacity Building: Reshaping Urban Community College Resources in Response to Emerging Challenges

Wright L. Lassiter, Jr.

Urban community colleges face evolving challenges in technology, commerce, politics, and demographics over the next decade, requiring a new and transformative paradigm. Emerging signposts point to expectations of personalized educational pathways, job-relevant knowledge and skills, global integration, and economic alignment. At the same time, however, colleges are struggling with limited and increasingly constrained resources.

States are spending 28% less per student in 2013 than they did in 2008, according to a report by the Center on Budget and Policy Priorities using data from the annual *Grapevine* study by Illinois State University (Oliff, Palacios, Johnson, & Leachman, 2013). The report notes that since the economic downturn that began in 2007, tuition has increased to compensate for those losses. As a result, the nonprofit think tank warns that it will be many years before states can again support colleges at prerecession levels. To rebuild their higher education systems, it urges more financial support rather than "shortsighted tax cuts that stifle higher education investments."

Regardless, college leaders must deliver better student services, greater workforce competency, and in the end enhanced value to society. In the past, solutions to most problems tended to involve more people, more processes, more time and more money. But more is sometimes just that—more, and not necessarily better. Innovation and future success will instead be

New Directions for Community Colleges, no. 162, Summer 2013 © 2013 Wiley Periodicals, Inc.
Published online in Wiley Online Library (wileyonlinelibrary.com) • DOI: 10.1002/cc.20062

guided by daring and increasingly entrepreneurial institutions. Their leaders must seek new revenue streams while aggressively containing costs. They must insist on better student-learning outcomes by creatively developing new approaches to educational opportunity and academic quality.

Sanford C. Shugart, president of Valencia Community College in Florida, shared this cogent view during a recent convocation at Cedar Valley College of the Dallas County Community College District (DCCCD):

> The challenge that we face as an industry is that we are being asked to achieve much better results with fewer resources to engage a needier student population, and we are caused to address challenges in an atmosphere of serious skepticism where all journalism is yellow, and our larger society no longer exempts our institutions (not us) from the deep distrust that has grown toward all institutions (Shugart, 2012).

In announcing a new initiative last year to educate an additional 5 million students by 2020, the American Association of Community Colleges noted that even while financial support for higher education has sharply declined, its direct link to American prosperity is greater than ever:

> Furthermore, education historically has not been a partisan issue, because national leaders typically have understood that the more educated people are, the more likely they are to be employed, earning a decent living, capable of supporting a family, paying taxes, contributing to the community, and participating in the democratic life of the nation (AACC, 2012, p. vii).

The record of accomplishment clearly speaks for itself, in that community colleges now enroll more than 13 million students in credit and noncredit courses and programs annually. They have prepared millions for careers and upper-division transfers. They have wholeheartedly responded to the clarion call from President Obama for retreading the American workforce, training displaced workers, and helping develop new industries. It is a record of success worthy of adoration and pride. But the real question today is whether our record will be similarly judged in the future.

Student Success and the Performance-Based Funding Challenge

Urban community colleges are at the vortex of the student success agenda that has dominated educational reform for several years. Without a massive overhaul of how institutions do business, jobs will be unfilled or lost for lack of skilled workers, and the country will continue to lose its edge in global competitiveness. In addition to the steady decline of state funding, fluctuations in the local property tax base of community colleges have also resulted in major financial losses. This has contributed to rising tuition, declining financial aid, and even program closures. Some have discussed curtailing or eliminating developmental education, which would in effect disqualify more than a third of today's students from attending college, because the cost is deemed too great for the benefit. Even as states continue to spend less on higher education every year, they are requiring more of community colleges and rewarding those that show improvement on a variety of measures. In short, we are competing for fewer dollars based on progress and completion as well as enrollment.

Each year, it becomes increasingly difficult to plan and budget for a new economy and rising expectations of success. Nowhere is this challenge more pressing than in community colleges expected to provide multiple constituencies with everything from highly technical customized job training to general university transfers.

What started out as a success and completion agenda has now become an accountability mandate causing college leaders to ask key questions: How do we make sound decisions in the best interest of our students and communities while managing an ever tighter budget? How do we position ourselves to better compete for limited resources? How do we leverage progress and success so that they count for something when states hand out funding?

A strong student success and completion agenda aligns well with performance-funding goals. Governing boards, CEOs, and key staff of urban/metropolitan community colleges who understand this can position their institutions to meet the challenge.

What Is the Response?

For colleges expected to do so much more with so much less, the financial future is daunting. The general public is most concerned about skyrocketing tuition costs, regardless of energy expenses, unfunded mandates, repair and renovation, personnel, or expanded service demands. Temporary federal stimulus dollars are gone, future cuts in state support are likely, and additional reductions in federal financial aid are on the horizon. Relief can only be expected from within.

Information technology can help cut costs and improve productivity by forming the best possible insights and decisions. Much more than collecting data and generating reports, analytics reveal problems, alert the institution to necessary action, unearth trends, reveal why the problem exists, and predict the success of various strategies.

Whether they are in the business or social sector, institutions aspiring to greatness must be realistic, disciplined and persistent, observes Jim Collins, writer of a series of books on "moving from good to great" (Collins, 2005). Instead of dismissing difficult or unpleasant data in higher education, we must face the wakeup call by using information technology to reduce costs, improve value, provide evidence and leverage innovation.

NEW DIRECTIONS FOR COMMUNITY COLLEGES • DOI: 10.1002/cc

Organizational Onion: One District's Reaction to Budgetary Realities

No institution easily deals with the loss of $33 million in revenue over two years while accommodating 20% enrollment growth. But an interesting series of strategies in reaction to just such a reality at DCCCD could serve as a guide for others:

> Given the weak economy, administrators planned for a 5 percent reduction in state funding in the 2010–2011 academic year. The actual reduction ballooned to more than 7.5 percent, an additional $13 million that DCCCD would be forced to do without. The cutbacks scuttled some planned investments. But educators took solace in knowing they would avoid layoffs—for now. (Joch, 2011, p. 33).

DCCCD took another $18 million hit as expected the following fall, "leaving critics to wonder just how much more the district can take" (Joch, 2011, p. 33).

"At some point, you can't throw another cup of water in the gumbo and expect to feed everyone at the table," said Edward DesPlas, DCCCD executive vice chancellor of business affairs (Joch, 2011).

Clearly this is more than just some postrecession hangover. Colleges are facing a seismic shift in funding that will profoundly alter how they apply for, receive, and use public and private dollars for years to come. Survival requires a number of tough choices.

The DCCCD chief financial officer and executive vice chancellor for business affairs, Edward DesPlas, dealt with it by working in concert with the DCC District Vice Presidents for Business Council. They crafted what was termed the "operational budget onion" as a vehicle for identifying and addressing budget and service priorities. This model will not only address the financial, human relations, service and student/success completion agenda, but also provides a framework for long-range financial planning.

As articulated by DesPlas, when faced with massive resource declines, as an alternative to across-the-board cuts we are better served by focusing on operational priorities. It can help to view the organization as an onion with multiple layers surrounding its core.

For colleges, of course, the core of operation is instruction. Its basic elements are students and the instructor. The classroom could be owned, borrowed, or rented. It could be bricks and mortar or virtual. But the core of college business exists in connecting students and instructors in pursuit of learning.

The first layer around the core is comprised of the services that connect students and instructors, create a safe environment, and attend to basic business functions that enable the college to remain a going concern.

NEW DIRECTIONS FOR COMMUNITY COLLEGES • DOI: 10.1002/cc

Those layers are human resources and business, admissions and assessment, advising, financial aid, learning resources, and campus security.

Moving toward the outside of the onion, the next layer consists of functions that support what is happening in the core and the first layer. This operational layer ensures the long-term success of the college and its mission. It includes accreditation, government requirements, facilities, and technology.

By now, one has an idea of how an organizational or budget onion can be drawn. The outer layers will look different based on different organizational priorities. However, the closer one gets to the core, the more similar these layers may look. As revenue declines, colleges can peel off outer layers to protect the core.

DesPlas offers this one caveat: The core is not immune from reductions, as instructional operations also lend themselves to budgetary and priority stratification. In other words, the core can become an onion unto itself.

The Dallas-Sized Budget Condition

The Dallas district is funded from three major sources: state appropriations (which have steadily declined from a high of 83% in 1985 to 29% of total operations in 2011), property taxes, and tuition. The latter was increased by 5% in 2012 after property tax revenue fell by a similar amount due to declining property values. The district has thus faced three consecutive years of heavy cuts amounting to $33 million in an annual operating budget of $407 million.

Meanwhile, enrollment has grown by more than 20% during the past five years to 41,500 credit students at the district's three urban colleges and another 43,700 at four others. There is a substantial backlog of deferred maintenance on older facilities at all seven colleges. And we have increased our physical "footprint" by one-third with the construction of 28 new facilities under a $450 million bond issue approved by voters in 2004 to accommodate enrollment growth projected to exceed a total of 83,000 credit students by 2015. Already, the district is serving more than 84,000 credit and an additional 25,000 continuing education and noncredit students. Three-quarters are nonwhite (37% Hispanic, 29% African American, and 8% Asian). Thus, our key function in a multiracial democracy is as apparent as our demographic diversity. But our institutional commitment to improving the graduation rate of 9% for those students is severely tested by a concurrent loss of resources.

Prior to the 2012–2013 fiscal year, it was not even possible to provide a cost-of-living adjustment to employees for three successive years. Faced with declines in revenue from two of three major sources, the district had to adjust for $33 million in overall resource reductions. Enacting across-the-board budget cuts in the face of enrollment growth and increased demand for services was not an option.

The CFO approached the chancellor with a bold initiative—voluntary retirement incentives to all employees 65 and older with 10 years of service, or age plus service equaling 80. The program consisted of two phases. In the first phase, eligible employees were offered 80% of base salary to retire within a year. In the second phase, eligible employees were offered 50% of base salary to retire by January 2012.

Of 677 eligible employees, 274 elected to participate in both phases of the program, at a buyout cost of $11.8 million and savings of $17.1 million through FY 2014 for a net gain of $5.3 million. A total of 73 positions were removed from organizational charts—24 administrators and 49 professional support staff. No faculty positions were eliminated, as savings would result from replacements employed at lower salaries.

Boosting Student Services with Financial Aid System Efficiency

The Dallas district has instituted a variety of other measures to address major shifts in revenue, including one with the objective of organizational efficiency following the 2009–2010 academic year. The U.S. Department of Education's requirement that colleges verify the identity of prospective students created an overwhelming amount of work. In 2009–2010, the district processed nearly 60,000 financial-aid applications, 40% of which were selected for verification. That meant 24,000 students had to print forms, copy tax returns, complete worksheets, and then fax, mail, or hand in other materials to confirm their identity and financial details.

Because of the amount of paperwork, and the fact that more than half of the verification forms were completed incorrectly, financial aid staff was fighting an uphill battle. Lines of students stretched out the doors of seven colleges as staff members met individually with students, answered constant phone calls and dealt with compliance issues. Reviewing files manually for verification took six to eight weeks, delaying financial aid awards. Student dissatisfaction was high. "We never had enough manpower to complete the work that had to be done," said Sharon Blackman, provost for educational affairs.

In 2010, a review of internal business processes led to the opportunity for change. Recognizing the need for a technology solution, the financial aid office worked with purchasing to find a qualified vendor to partner with.

Global Financial Aid Services Inc. was determined to have the technological answer for this massive problem with its Global-CORE + File Review product. Work began on implementation in July 2011. While an off-the-shelf system was selected, custom enhancements were added. The new system, which looks nothing like its former self, included an online student portal branded to DCCCD, automatic student email notifications, paperless document collection, and an interface for college staff to monitor student status, check documents, and run reports.

In 15 minutes, students can complete an online form, which increases filing accuracy, and click to request IRS documents to be forwarded to their college directly. If information entered conflicts with what they previously reported, they are notified in real-time. The entire process is paperless. The compliance review portion was also outsourced with results compiled and communicated to DCCCD daily.

As a result, the file review time for students selected for verification has been reduced from eight weeks to five days. More importantly, staff members can now devote themselves to counseling rather than paperwork review, which allows them to help more first-time students, who typically need more advising. Focusing on at-risk students results in increased retention and higher graduation rates. Staff resources were redeployed to a new centralized contact center, which reduced the need for seasonal hiring.

With two years' data now available, DCCCD is looking at conducting predictive modeling to identify applicant trends and plan strategy for the upcoming academic year. Implementation of this paperless system resulted in Dallas being one of nine colleges and universities nationwide recognized by *University Business* magazine in its winter 2012 "Models of Efficiency" program for innovative approaches to streamline higher education operations.

"Student satisfaction and retention is key for any higher education institution, and the Dallas online financial verification portal addresses that well," said Tim Goral, editor in chief of *University Business* in announcing the award. "Dallas went beyond federal compliance to make a project easier and more efficient for all parties involved." Given those gains in service and efficiency, the real price of the new system was cost-neutral.

Evaluation and Efficiency: Protecting the Core

Now is the time for innovative and creative leaders to engage in the necessary process of evaluating organizational efficiency and effectiveness. Search out problems *before* something breaks. Encourage staff and stakeholders to identify possible areas of improvement and savings. Look at what others have done. By always seeking new ways to peel the onion down to the core if need be, we invariably find both incremental and transformative enhancements to ensure the sustained viability of our institutions and the communities we serve.

References

AACC (2012, April). *Reclaiming the American dream: Community colleges and the nation's future.* A Report from the 21st Century Commission on the Future of Community Colleges. American Association of Community Colleges. Retrieved from www.aacc .nche.edu/aboutcc/21stcenturyreport/21stCenturyReport.pdf

Collins, J. (2005). *Good to great and the social sectors: Why business thinking is not the answer* (excerpts). Retrieved from www.jimcollins.com/books/g2g-ss.html

Joch, A. (2011, June/July). Going lean. *Community College Journal*. Retrieved from www .ccjournal-digital.com/ccjournal/20110607?pg=3#pg34

Oliff, P., Palacios, V., Johnson, I., & Leachman, M. (2013, March 19). *Recent deep state higher education cuts may harm students and the economy for years to come*. Center on Budget and Policy Priorities. www.cbpp.org/cms/index.cfm?fa=view&id=3927

Shugart, S. (September 2012). Recorded by author, Lanacster, Texas. Opening convocation, Cedar Valley College.

WRIGHT L. LASSITER, JR., *plans to retire early next year as chancellor of the seven-college Dallas County Community College District, a position he has held since 2006. He previously served for 20 years as president of DCCCD's El Centro College. He was described by the Dallas Morning News in 2010 as "one of the humble yet towering pillars in higher education and religion in Dallas."*

NEW DIRECTIONS FOR COMMUNITY COLLEGES • DOI: 10.1002/cc

The term "community college business and finance model" is unlikely to evoke a positive response from educators who resist labeling students as "customers," do not want to call the college's offerings "products," and don't like to hear the college referred to as a "business." Faculty and staff tend to be conservative and risk-averse when confronted with major institutional changes that they feel diminish the distinctiveness of the college, its academic freedom, their special relationship with students, and obligation to the public good. These are all valid concerns. But they should guide rather than deter the necessary transformation of business and finance operations to become leaner, smarter, more efficient, more creative, and more focused in response to new financial constraints and changing demographic, economic, technological, and social realities.

The New Community College Business and Finance Model

Gunder Myran

We are all familiar with the old canard that the railroads failed because they thought they were in the railroad business when in fact they were in the transportation business. By the time they discovered this, they had been overtaken by the airlines and other transportation modes. Examples of industries that had to create new business models in response to changing global and technological realities include the steel industry, health care, and automakers. In this same light, community colleges have for too long assumed they are in the campus/classroom business when in fact they need to be in the learning and talent development business. This chapter explores the challenges, processes, and best practices of such a new business and finance model.

The term *business and finance model* is used instead of the more common *business model* here because community college professionals tend to think that the latter refers only to financial management functions. The impact of the new model is much deeper and broader as indicated by these definitions: The *business dimension* refers to the product development (advancement of the curriculum, student services, continuing education, workforce development, and the like) and the planning, organizing, staffing, evaluation, and other processes of the college. The *finance dimension* refers to the management and development of human, financial, physical, technological, and information resources.

New Financial Realities and the Social Equity Agenda

As a result of economic decline and the collapse of property values during the recent "great recession," community colleges have faced dramatic reductions in state aid and local property tax support. It is expected that an era of significantly reduced revenue will persist into the foreseeable future. Nearly all community colleges have been negatively affected by the closing of factories and other businesses, increased unemployment, and other consequences of the recent economic downturn. Urban centers are particularly hard hit due to pre-existing disparities in income, employment, and educational opportunities. The uneven impact highlights the magnitude of an unfinished multiracial democracy. The passion to address these disparities has ignited the "fire in the belly" of urban community college leaders as they strive to achieve a social equity agenda while also adapting the business and finance dimensions of their colleges to new financial realities.

Lessons Learned from For-Profit Colleges

A recent article by JoAnna Schilling in *Community College Journal of Research and Practice* suggests that community colleges can learn from the business models of for-profit colleges. Schilling says community college leaders are dismissive of for-profit colleges because they perceive them as having dismal degree completion rates, being too heavily focused on skills-based training, exploiting minority and low-income students, and inappropriately funded by federal financial aid. Nevertheless, she proposes that community colleges can learn from the more flexible, customer-service orientation of the for-profit business model. She points in particular to their continuous curriculum updates, streamlined admissions, entrepreneurial management, more focused academic curricula, active employer advisory practices, diverse delivery methods, and annual program audits (Schilling, 2013, pp. 153–159).

The Old Community College Business and Finance Model

Community colleges have operated in the past on a business and finance model designed to create value based on traditional assumptions such as low tuition, little or no private funding, and slow curriculum development within program and discipline silos. A large number of career education and continuing education programs are offered, but they are often criticized as "a mile wide and an inch deep." Innovation has been largely based on faculty and staff preferences, campus-based delivery of educational programs and services, local face-to-face constituencies, and separate credit and noncredit offerings. Decision making was internally focused and intuitive, relying on rules and hierarchy rather than evidence and outcomes. The mode of teaching and learning was "one size fits all." While these practices have served the college well enough for decades, it is time to "jump the S-curve" to a new future-oriented model.

Jumping the S-Curve: Forces Driving the New Business and Finance Model

The old community college business model is increasingly obsolete and dysfunctional in the face of fast-changing demographic, economic, cultural, and technological conditions. State funding is in a long-term trend of disinvestment. There is growing concern about intrusive regulations and demands for greater accountability from government, massive student debt, public skepticism about the value of higher education, state-level performance-based funding models, and declining or stagnant student enrollment. Rising legacy costs, aging infrastructure, and competition from for-profit institutions and other colleges drain resources even further, as do employee health insurance costs and labor contracts. As these fast-changing conditions overwhelm the old business and finance model, transition to a new one begins.

A modern version of the old organizational life cycle (ascend, plateau, and then either reinvent or decline) is the *S-curve*. Organizations follow an S-curve as they mature: Market relevance ebbs, the distinctiveness of their capabilities declines and talent development slows. High-performing organizations "jump the S-curve" to a new business model before the old one starts to stall. In other words, they focus on fixing what doesn't appear to be broken (Nunes & Breene, 2012, pp. 80–87).

The classroom-based, fixed-place, semester-length course mode of most community colleges requires students to lead double lives—one a virtual world where they design and participate in their own learning endeavors, and the other the "one size fits all" world of the typical community college. Top-performing colleges recognize this, and jump the S-curve—invent a new business model—even while it may appear to others that the old model is still working just fine.

The Community College Strategic Development Framework

The business and finance model of a community college is an integral dimension of its strategic development framework, outlined as follows:

- *Foundational Statements*: mission statement (the college's social purpose), values statement (a declaration of the beliefs to which the faculty and staff are committed), functions statement (how the mission will be achieved), and the service area and key constituencies statements.
- *Vision Statement*: A condensed statement of the preferred future to which all associated with the college will devote their talents and energies.
- *Institutional Strategy*: An integrated and holistic set of decisions that charts the future course of the college and creates an institutional environment for the successful execution of the mission and vision (Myran, Baker, Simone, & Zeiss, 2003, p. 3).
- *Business and Finance Model*: A blueprint or roadmap for how the college will advance its mission and achieve its strategies. It is designed to create and deliver value for student, business, and community customers while adding value to the college. The model has four interlocking elements:
  - Element One: Customer Value Proposition (CVP)
    The CVP describes how the college will create value for its student, business, and community customers. Community colleges face the challenge of providing the right mix of programs and services that add value in the lives of customers while also dealing with constrained financial resources and demands for accountability. Harvard Business School's Robert Kaplan and David Norton define CVP as the "unique mix of product, price, service, relationship, and image that a company offers. It defines how the organization differentiates itself from competitors to attract, retain, and deepen relationships with targeted customers. The customer value proposition is crucial because it helps an organization connect its internal processes to improved outcomes for its customers" (Kaplan & Norton, 2001, p. 93).
    Examples of community college CVPs include qualification for a good job and career advancement; opportunity to earn a college-level degree or certificate; credentialing of student achievements (grades, portfolios, certificates, and degrees); affordability; and increased student employability and earning power.
  - Element Two: Value Network or Chain
    The value chain or network is how the college establishes its customer value proposition in cooperation with community partners, supporters, vendors, legislators, regulators, and other key stakeholders.
  - Element Three: College Resources and Processes
    Resource management in the new business model refers to the orchestration and development of faculty and staff talents, as well as financial, physical, technological, and information assets to maximize the value added for customers. *Process* management orchestrates areas such as staff professional development, program and service improvement, strategic and annual planning, and budget production in a way that also maximizes the value added for college customers.

- Element Four: Financial Strategy
  An effective business and finance model adds value to both the college and customer by providing a strategic margin between revenue and cost for investment in future development.

The first two elements of this business and finance model, CVP and value networks, primarily add value for the customer; the last two, college resources/processes and financial strategy, add value to the college as well (Sheets, Crawford, & Soares, 2012, pp. 1–5). The college activates these two elements by achieving productivity, quality and financial sustainability objectives.

A condensed version of the new performance-based community college business and finance model is provided by the Lumina Foundation's higher education strategic plan for 2013–2016. It calls for strong incentives for affordability and completion; increased attainment by underrepresented students; expanded capacity to deliver high-quality, low-cost educational programs; reduced time and credits required for degree completion; solutions to workforce shortages in high-demand fields; and improved productivity (Lumina Foundation, 2013, p. 18).

Creating a new model is a major strategic undertaking for community colleges. The transition requires transformation of organizational capabilities, structures, and processes. It means delivering greater value to an expanded range of customers, including individuals with diverse personal needs as well as businesses and communities in the service region. Ultimately, it means changing the organizational culture in a fundamental way.

In recent years, the City College of San Francisco has struggled against an organizational culture resistant to change while striving to reinvent itself amid major financial, accreditation, and political issues. In an era of reduced resources and increased accountability, inability or unwillingness to change is a recipe for failure. Thelma Scott-Skillman, interim chancellor and a member of the CCSF "Back from the Cliff" panel charged with reinventing the college, observed in *Community College Week* that "It takes time for a cultural change to get interlocked with the new way of doing business."

Disruptive Innovations

Transitioning to a new business and finance model requires what Harvard Professor Clayton Christensen called "disruptive innovations" that improve a product or service in a way that creates new markets in place of existing ones. These new solutions gradually improve to the point where they overtake previously dominant practices (Sheets et al., 2012, p. 2). In the case of the community college, disruptive innovations include new community partnerships, college and career readiness programs, more structured and limited pathways from student entry to completion, online learning, computer-enhanced learning modules, hybrid classrooms and digitally based instruction, flipped classrooms, accelerated developmental education, dual enrollment of high school students, acceleration of certificate and degree completion, massive open online courses, first-year experience programs, and the merging of credit and noncredit programming.

Community colleges in some states are considering privatization—moving away from the intrusive restrictions of state-level regulations and funding. An excellent example of a disruptive innovation is the New Community College in midtown Manhattan, built from the ground up with a totally new way of doing business. Students must attend full-time, remedial work is imbedded in credit coursework, and there are limited and well-defined pathways to a degree. Another example is the building of new dormitories at Jackson Community College (Michigan) to increase enrollment, generate revenue, and compete with other regional colleges. Hagerstown Community College (Maryland) is demonstrating disruptive innovation in leading a community-wide effort to attract biotechnology-, alternative energy-, cybersecurity-, and bioscience-related industries to Hagerstown and Washington County, with talent development and human capital as the primary economic engine. The project includes an economic development strategy in partnership with regional economic development, governmental, and educational entities; building a major STEM (science, technology, engineering, and mathematics) facility on campus; and expanding bioscience programming.

Activating the New Model

Listed below are some of the ways that community colleges are giving life to the new business and finance model. The business dimension (product development, planning, and other institutional processes) is followed by the finance dimension (developing and managing human, financial, physical, technological, and information resources).

Best Practices, Business Dimension

- Reduce cost to students through initiatives such as lessening the time it takes to complete a certificate or associate degree and providing free electronic educational content ("open educational resources").
- Shift to a shorter product development cycle so that continuous improvement of curricular and student services is an ongoing process of adaptation and transformation.
- Increase emphasis on measuring the effectiveness of every college function in terms of its contribution to student, business, and community success and satisfaction.
- Create simplified and more accessible solutions to the problems of individuals, businesses, and communities.

NEW DIRECTIONS FOR COMMUNITY COLLEGES • DOI: 10.1002/cc

- Increase capacity to provide affordable, high-quality education to a greater number of students, with a focus on serving low-income and minority individuals.
- Create innovative, high-quality, and lower-cost means of instructional delivery.
- Expand performance-based funding of programs and services.
- Strengthen program review processes and program cost models.
- Invest in high-demand career fields (greater emphasis on data-informed continuous improvement of career and workforce education programming in response to changing workforce trends and skill requirements).
- Expand business and other community partnerships that result in shared mission and cost initiatives.
- Develop a predictive analytical model for strategic and annual planning using "big data" and learning analytics approaches.
- Emphasize the college's distinctiveness compared to other service providers to combat the "commoditization" of higher education (customers seeing higher education services as commodities and all providers as the same).
- Refine data management policies and procedures regarding the design, collection, analysis, reporting and distribution of institutional statistics and student performance data to internal and external users.

Best Practices, Finance Dimension

- Emphasize nontraditional funding alternatives, such as private fundraising and creating profit centers through public access to college Internet cafes, bookstores, food service, and other services.
- Build the capacity of faculty and staff to be more productive through professional development programs, curricular redesign, and reassignment.
- Target human, financial, physical, information, and technology resources in student completion and other highest-priority institutional goals.
- Focus on achieving greater impact of each dollar expended through continuous improvement of the effectiveness and efficiency of services and processes.
- Increase transparency and accountability based on the quantification of the value of every investment in programs, services, facilities, and other college functions.
- Shift from a low-tuition strategy to multitiered tuition pattern coupled with greater financial aid for low-income students.
- Strengthen internal audit practices that facilitate performance and productivity review, data-driven decisions, and performance reporting.
- Create multiyear financial planning and budgeting processes.
- Strengthen financial accounting and analysis processes, including financial forecasting and performance-based funding systems.

Perceptions of Community College Leaders

In 2012, four students (Lilly Anderson, Sue De Camillis, Fiona Hert, and Jan Karazim) in the Doctorate in Community College Leadership at Ferris State University (Michigan) interviewed a number of community college leaders to get their insights about the emerging business and finance model. Selected comments from those interviews offer relevant perspective on the subject:

Walter Bumphus, president and CEO, American Association of Community Colleges (AACC): "I think that the metrics by which we measure student success are the key to the whole process. We would like to think that the VFA (Voluntary Framework on Accountability sponsored by AACC and the Association of Community College Trustees) will be the metric that will be used."

George Boggs, president and CEO emeritus, AACC: "The topic of customer value is becoming more prominent with a couple of different drivers. One of course is the fact that President Obama has challenged us to improve our college completion rates and once again make our country more competitive economically and educationally. This has happened at the same time that the economic recession hit; hence, colleges are trying to figure out how to do a better job of improving college completion even though they have fewer resources to do so."

Jerry Sue Thornton, president, Cuyahoga Community College (Ohio): "I think a new business model is emerging. The governors are causing it to emerge. Funding from the states is pushing the agenda. Think about the states that have had tremendous funding cutbacks such as California. The cuts are so deep that they are really restructuring our institutions. However, I wouldn't use the word *business* and the word *customer* in working with the faculty. They resent the idea that there would be a comparison between education and business."

Joe May, president of the Louisiana State Community College System: The new business model is "all about the voice of the customer. It is not about us; we are a means to an end for our students. In the old business model, we basically put the programs and courses out there and made them available at a time and place we determined. In the new business model, we need to have the mind-set of problem solvers. We need to get inside the problems of the student and remove every barrier, every problem that makes it hard for them to succeed. We must also meet the students where they are, whether it involves low income, limited literacy skills, lack of job skills, or personal issues in legal, custody, and welfare areas."

Gerardo de los Santos, president and CEO, League for Innovation in the Community College: "Our current business model, if you want to break it down into its most fundamental rubrics, is payment for courses. That's as basic as it gets. I believe there are signs of new business models out there. Think about what is happening through the leveraging of technology with instructional delivery options such as open source. If community college faculty and students are going to have access to very highly sophisticated, high-quality courses that are free and continue to propagate, then what does that say for the emerging business model in higher education?"

Tim Nelson, president of Northwestern Michigan College: "When you ask what the new business model is, I think you are asking the wrong question. The real question you should ask is 'What is the customer value proposition (CVP)?' You start with the question, 'What is causing people to do business with you in the first place?' The CVP is related to the high purpose of gaining the skills and experience that will help our learners create economic and social wealth during their life's journey. It's about talent, not the degree. The community college value proposition is to create a talented population."

Terry O'Banion, former president and CEO, League for Innovation in the Community College: "The idea of customer service is a sound principle coming out of business. It is very adaptable and does work in an educational environment, but the faculty doesn't like that language. Because of the vast differences in culture, I don't think you can transfer a business model into the educational culture."

Reality Check: A District Design Initiative

In 2006, Wayne County Community College District (WCCCD), with more than 70,000 credit and noncredit students at five campuses around the metropolitan Detroit region, was already suffering the early recessionary impact of a rapid and dramatic decline in two of its three primary revenue sources—local property taxes and state aid. The long-term outlook was equally bleak.

State appropriations for the 43 public colleges and universities in Michigan are the same $1.6 billion today as they were 20 years ago, according to the nationwide *Grapevine* study of fiscal support for higher education (*Grapevine*, 2012–2013). Meanwhile, the state's share of operating costs at 28 community colleges has fallen from roughly 33% in 1994–1995 to 19% today, leaving the colleges, their local property-tax payers, and their students to make up the difference. As a result, tuition and fees have gone from a third to nearly half of the whole in Michigan, while property taxes have remained fairly constant at 32%.

In Detroit, where 36% of the population lives in poverty, voters have nonetheless stepped up repeatedly to support six WCCCD millage renewals or increases since 1994 including a major hike in 2001. Following the 2001 support, the WCCCD Pathways to the Future initiative was launched, spending approximately $150 million during its "jump-start" period to transform programs, services, facilities, learning, and information systems throughout the district. WCCCD also experienced the biggest percentage credit enrollment growth of any similar urban system in the country over the same 10-year period. Then property values crashed by more than half, and the district was looking at a $25 million budget shortfall—nearly a quarter of its operating revenue. In 2012, voters narrowly approved another millage increase to recover a portion of these lost funds.

It also helped that a new business and finance model was already in place thanks to the WCCCD District Design Initiative (DDI), launched in 2010 as the primary mechanism for balancing student success and financial sustainability objectives in anticipation of long-term financial constraints. Sustainability is now being achieved by six major agendas:

- *Financial Sustainability Agenda*: Moving over a multiyear period to a financial condition in which total expenditures match reduced revenue levels while minimizing the negative impact on student learning by redirecting resources to the success/completion agenda and other highest priority institutional development projects.
- *Productivity Agenda*: Undertaking program reviews, expanded internal audits, financial controls, cost-benefit studies, and other transparency and accountability measures to maximize the impact on student success for each dollar invested.
- *Capacity Agenda*: Maximizing the impact of resource capacity (human, financial, physical, information, and technological) on achievement of the district's mission, vision, and goals.
- *Institutional Redesign Agenda*: Redesigning programs, services, structures, and processes to increase efficiency, effectiveness, and impact on student success and completion.
- *Student Success/Completion Agenda (WCCCD Student Completion 2020)*: Redirecting resources, in light of reduced funds, on the highest priority—continuously increasing course, program, certificate, and degree completions.
- *National Community College Engagement Agenda*: Participating in national community college initiatives that relate to productivity and student completion.

A Program Cost and Review Model: Central Piedmont Community College

When Central Piedmont Community College (North Carolina) experienced a $20 million loss in state aid at the height of the recent economic downturn, it upgraded its program review and cost model to achieve the dual goals of cost containment and quality. A formal review of each instructional program is conducted every five years with a midpoint review at the end of two and one-half years. All service units are reviewed every three years. Programs are assessed against core indicators such as demand, high/low cost factors, student completion and dropout rates, enrollment trends, and the employment patterns of graduates. In addition, a college-wide cost study is conducted every two years to develop an in-depth understanding of direct and indirect costs for each program and service in relation to customer outcomes, cost efficiency, and relative need for investment or disinvestment. The benefits of the program cost and review models are:

- Faculty and staff collaboration on data collection for program and service decisions
- Increased awareness by faculty and staff of the impact of cost factors on program decisions
- Increased use of student performance and financial trends data to make decisions
- Increased entrepreneurship among faculty and staff as they explore alternative sources of revenue
- Increased understanding by employers of the value of financially supporting beneficial programs
- Improved alignment between program costs and planning/budget decisions (Hert, 2013)

Infusing New Model with Democratic Values

There are a number of preconditions for the successful launch of a new business and finance model. The president and executive team must be skilled in leading the reinvention of institutional programs, services, structures, and processes required to adapt to the financial, economic, demographic, and cultural trajectory of community colleges that we now call the "new normal." The updated model requires a spirit of entrepreneurship and risk-taking at all levels of the college, which must also have talented persons in key decision roles who can project a change strategy and build consensus and teamwork around it. Finally, there must be an institutional culture of trust, transparency, collaboration, and teamwork.

With these conditions in place, community colleges can successfully navigate turbulent times to achieve the noble outcomes of economic well-being for their citizens, meaning a public life informed by justice, equity, and social responsibility. Far from emulating for-profit colleges or business enterprises, the new community college business and finance model is guided—as always—by a fierce commitment to a singular mission and set of values. As they move from a campus/classroom model to a learning and talent development model, urban colleges lead the way in infusing the new design with a social equity imperative that will uplift and advance the egalitarian and democratic ideals of these unique institutions.

NEW DIRECTIONS FOR COMMUNITY COLLEGES • DOI: 10.1002/cc

References

Grapevine (2013). Center for the Study of Education Policy at Illinois State University. Summary Tables FY 2012–13 and Historical Data, 1994–95. Retrieved from http://grapevine.illinoisstate.edu/tables/index.htm

Hert, F. (2013). *Increasing efficiencies and effectiveness in community colleges.* (Unpublished doctoral dissertation). Ferris State University, Michigan.

Myran, G., Baker, G., Simone, B., & Zeiss, T. (2003). *Leadership strategies for community college executives.* Washington, DC: Community College Press, American Association of Community Colleges.

Nunes, P., & Breene, T. (2012). Reinvent your business before it's too late. *Harvard Business Review,* January/February.

Kaplan, R. S., & Norton, D. P. (2001). *The strategy-focused organization.* Boston, MA: Harvard Business School Press.

Lumina Foundation (2013). *Strategic plan, 2013–2016.* Retrieved from www.luminafoundation.org/advantage/document/goal_2025/2013-Lumina_Strategic_Plan.pdf

Schilling, J. (2013). What's money got to do with it? The appeal of the for-profit education model. *Community College Journal of Research and Practice,* 37(3).

Sheets, R., Crawford, S., & Soares, L. (2012, March 28). *Rethinking higher education business models.* Center for American Progress and EDUCAUSE.

GUNDER MYRAN *is president emeritus of Washtenaw Community College in Ann Arbor, Michigan. Prior to his 23-year tenure as WCC's president, he served as a professor in administration and higher education in the College of Education at Michigan State University. He is also a faculty member and national advisory board member of the Doctorate in Community College Leadership at Ferris State University.*

NEW DIRECTIONS FOR COMMUNITY COLLEGES • DOI: 10.1002/cc

INDEX

Accelerated Study in Associate Programs (ASAP; CUNY), 23–24
ACCT. *See* Association of Community College Trustees (ACCT)
ACE. *See* Achieving a College Education
ACE Native Americans, 82
Achieving a College Education (ACE), 81–82
Achieving the Dream Inc., 28, 52
Achieving the Dream Leader College, 23
Achua, C. F., 32–33
ACT, 70
Adult ACE program, 82
Aerospace Institute (St. Louis Community College), 60
AGB. *See* Association of Governing Boards of Universities and Colleges (AGB)
Age of Enlightenment, 20
Alamo district (Texas), 38
American Association of Community Colleges (AACC), 1, 12–14, 22, 30–31, 39–41, 56, 76, 86, 100; and campus wide inclusiveness, 15; and community engagement, 15; and reclaiming American Dream, 13–14; and reinventing open door, 14; and student access, 14; and student success, 14
American Association of Junior Colleges (American Association of Community Colleges), 1
American Association of University Professors (AAUP), 39
American Council on Education, 9
American Dream, reclaiming, 13–14
American Dream Updated (American Association of Junior Colleges), 1
"America's Urban Crisis," 16
Anderson, L., 100
Arkansas, 55
Asian Pacific Islanders Association, 79
Aspen Prize for Community College Excellence, 24
Association of American Colleges and Universities (AAC&U), 66–67
Association of Chicanos for Higher Education, 79

Association of Community College Trustees (ACCT), 31, 32, 38, 76–77
Association of Governing Boards of Universities and Colleges (AGB), 39
Ayers, D., 75, 76

Baker, G., 57, 96
Baltimore City Community College (BCCC; Maryland), 3, 37, 40, 51
Bank of America, 71
Barlett v. Strickland, 21
Bassett, J. A., 2, 8, 11, 21, 22, 33, 48, 64
BCCC. *See* Baltimore City Community College
Berger, P. L., 38
Bill and Melinda Gates Foundation, 3; Completion by Design program, 70
Board of Education, Brown v., 63
Boeing Defense, Space, and Security, 59, 60
Boggs, G. R., 30–31, 100
Bolman, L. G., 33, 34, 43
Boyatzis, R. E., 31
Breaking Through, 52
Breene, T., 95
Brown v. Board of Education, 63
Bumphus, W., 1–2, 100

Campuswide inclusiveness, 15
Capacity building: and boosting student services with financial aid system efficiency, 90–91; and Dallas County Community College District, 88–90; and nature of response, 87; and reshaping urban community college resources in response to emerging challenges, 85–91; and student success and performance-based funding challenge, 86–87
Career education: emerging themes of, 48–49; and workforce development, 46; and workforce development practices, 51–52
Carnevale, A., 45–47
Cedar Valley College (Dallas County Community College District), 86
Center for Male Engagement (Community College of Philadelphia), 52

Center on Budget and Policy Priorities, 85
Central Piedmont Community College (North Carolina), 12, 102
Change: The Magazine of Higher Learning (Miller), 28
Charles Kennedy Equity Award, 77
Chattanooga State Community College (CSCC; Tennessee), 51
Christensen, C., 97
"Circle of Life" (Native American philosophy), 80
City College of San Francisco, 38, 97
City Colleges of Chicago, 52
City University of New York (CUNY), 10; Accelerated Study in Associate Programs (ASAP), 23–24
Cleveland Metropolitan School District, 57, 58
Cohen, A. M., 63
College Board, 69
College Board Advanced Placement, 58
College completion imperative, advancing economic equity and, 9–10
Collins, J., 88
Columbia University, 22; Teachers College Center for Benefit-Cost Studies of Education, 24
COMBASE consortium, 12–14
Commission on the Future of Community Colleges (AACU), 52
Community College Journal of Research and Practice, 94
Community College of Baltimore County, 37
Community College of Philadelphia (Pennsylvania), 52
Community College Week, 97
Community engagement, 15
Community partnerships: and Cuyahoga Community College's Early College High School, 57–59; and environmental risk factors compelling combined response, 56–57; reframing, 55–61; and selected best partnership practices, 57–60; and Sinclair Community College, 59; and St. Louis Community College, 59–60
Completion by Design (Gates Foundation), 3, 52, 70
Completion college, 15
Conrad, C., 29
Council on Black American Affairs, 79
Crawford, S., 97

Cross, K. P., 40
Cuba, revolution in, 63
Cuban immigrants, 64
Cuyahoga Community College, 57–59, 100; Design Lab Early College High School, 57–59

Dade County Junior College, 63, 64
Dallas County Community College District (DCCCD), 86, 88
Davis, B., 60
Davis, G., 41
Day One Guarantee (Louisiana Community and Technical College System), 52
Dayton Public Schools (Ohio), 59
DCCCD. *See* Dallas County Community College District
De Camillis, S., 100
de los Santos, G., 100–101
De Souza Briggs, X., 21
Deal, T. F., 43
Declaration of Independence, 2
Delta Coast Project, 22
Democracy Commitment Project (AACC), 22
Democracy's college, reframing, 16–17
DesPlas, E., 88
DeStefano, Ricci v., 21
Detroit, Michigan, 21–22, 47–48, 101
Disequilibrium, 30
Diversity Advancement Project (Kirwan Institute/Center for Social Inclusion), 22
Domino Brands, 51
Donohue, P. C., 27, 32
Drew, S., 56
DRS Sustainment Systems, 59
Drucker, P., 43, 57

Early College High School Initiative, 57
Early College High School Student Information System, 58
Economic equity, advancing, 9–10
Emerson Center for Engineering and Manufacturing (St. Louis Community College, Florissant Valley), 59
ENGAGE instrument (ACT), 70
Equality Maricopa, 79
Expressions Newsletter, 79–80

Ferris State University (Michigan), 100
Florida International University, 71
Florida State University, 64

Focused Learning System (Chattanooga State Community College), 51
Fuss, D., 26

Gallos, J. V., 33, 34
Garcia, E., 24
Gateway STEM High School (St. Louis, Missouri), 60
Gear Up, 52
George, A., 57
Georgetown University Center on Education and the Workforce, 45, 47, 72
Gillett-Karam, R., 3, 37
GKN Aerospace, 59, 60
Glasper, R., 3, 75
Glazer, L., 9
Gleazer, E., 1
Global Financial Aid Services Inc., 90
Global-CORE + File Review, 90
Goal 2025 (Lumina Foundation), 12–13
Goleman, D., 31
Gollattsheck, J. F., 40, 41
Goral, T., 91
Governing board: and being true to mission and values, 42–43; and current knowledge, 39–40; and emphasis on community and education, 40–41; future-shaping function of, 33–43; and governance guiding actions, 41; and opportunities and values defining governance, 38–39; and politics and power, 41–42; and ten recommendations for future governance, 43
Grapevine, 85, 93, 101
Gray, T. I., 56
Greater Miami Urban League (Florida), 64
Greenberg, E., 21
Grewal, E., 21
Guilford Area School Assistance Program (North Carolina), 52
Guilford Technical College (GTCC; North Carolina), 52
Gunder, M., 45

Haas Diversity Research Center (Berkeley), 22
Hager, C.J.E., 76
Hagerstown Community College (Maryland), 98
Hammond, C., 56
Harlacher, E. L., 40, 41
Hart, B., 75, 76

Harvard Business School, 96
Harvard University Open Collections Program, 46
HECTIC, 28
Hert, F., 100, 103
Hill-Collins, P., 38
Hines, T. E., 28, 31
Hispanic Access to College Education Resources project (¡HACER!), 71
Holley, D., 21
Hoop of Learning, 80
Hoover, E., 76
Houston Community College, 10
Hurst, M., 1, 2

Illinois State University, 85
Institute for Social Research, University of Michigan, 48
Integrated Postsecondary Education Data System (IPEDS), 10, 11
Ivery, C. L., 2, 3, 8, 11, 19, 21, 22, 33, 45, 48, 64

Jackson Community College (Michigan), 98
Jobs of the Future, 52
Joch, A., 88
Johns Hopkins Hospital and Health System, 51
Johnson, I., 85
Jr. ACE program, 82

Kalogrides, D., 21
Kanter, R. M., 32
Kaplan, R. S., 96
Karazim, J., 100
Kellogg Foundation, 1
King, M. L., Jr., 83
Kingsborough Community College (Brooklyn, N.Y.), 24
Kirwan, W., 9
Kirwan Institute for the Study of Race and Ethnicity, Ohio State University, 22
Knight Foundation, 70
Knowledge-based economy: community colleges as talent centers for, 9
Kresge Foundation, 70
Krysan, M., 21
Kucsera, J., 21

Lassiter, W. L., Jr., 3, 85
Lazarus, E., 43
Leachman, M., 85

Leadership, new paradigm for 21st century, 27–34; and change-supporting strategies, 32–33; and engaging changed mission, 31; and implementing promise of open door, 31–32; and nature of disequilibrium, 30; and people as leaders, 30–31; and reframing community college leadership, 33–34; and utility of synergy, 32; and what is truly essential for managing change, 29–30

League for Innovation in the Community College, 100–101

Learn to Earn, 52

Lee, J. M., Jr., 81

Levin, H., 24

Levin, J. S., 75, 82

Liberal Education and America's Promise (LEAP) initiative, 66–67, 71

Linton, D., 56

Los Angeles Community College District, 10

Los Angeles Times, 40

Louisiana, 55

Louisiana Community and Technical College System (LCTCS), 52

Louisiana State Community College System, 100

Luckmann, T., 38

Lumina Foundation, 10, 12–13, 27, 53, 70, 71, 97; and creating 21st-century higher education system, 13; and *Goal 2025,* 13; and mobilizing to reach *Goal 2025,* 13

Lussier, R. N., 32–33

Maathai, W., 16

Male Empowerment Network (MEN), 81

Maricopa Community Colleges (Arizona), 3, 10, 38, 75–83; Chancellor's Diversity Initiative, 78

Maricopa Diversity Advisory Council (DAC), 79

Maricopa Hoop of Learning program, 80

Matheny, C. J., 29

Mathis, M., 31

Maximizing Our Strengths as an Inclusive Community (MOSAIC), 79

May, J., 100

McClenney, B., 31

McKee, A., 31

Mercer Community College (New Jersey), 24

Miami, Florida, 64; Greater Miami Chamber of Commerce, 71

Miami Book Fair International, 66

Miami Dade College (MDC), 3, 10, 38, 63–72; and assessing culture of evidence, 68; and evolution of academic institution, 64–65; and expanding opportunities in urban context, 65–66; and learning outcomes: defining college education, 66; mapping curriculum at, 67–68; New World School of the Arts, 66; and persisting challenges, 68–69; School for Advanced Studies (SAS), 66; and sharing universal resource of higher education, 72; Student Achievement Initiatives (SAI), 69–70; and sustained improvements in student experience, 71–72; and ten liberal-learning outcomes, 66–67; and turning challenges into successes, 69–71

Miami International Film Festival, 66

Miami-Dade County (Florida), 63, 65; Public Schools, 66, 71

Michigan, 101

Michigan Future Inc., 9

Middle skill talent, 47, 53

Miller, M., 28–29

Milwaukee Area Technical College, 29

Minority Male Initiative (MMI), 80–81

Missouri Manufacturing Workforce Innovation Network, 51

"Models of Efficiency" (*University Business* magazine), 91

Morgan, J., 24

Morgan Stanley, 51

Morgan State University Community College Leadership Doctoral Program, 28

Mulkins-Manning, T., 30

Multiracial democracy: achieving, on campus, 75–83; and consensus emerging from national completion initiatives, 22–23; and CUNY's ASAP, 23–24; and new paradigm of education, 21–22; origins and definitions of, 19–20; and resegregation thwarting progress, 21; shaping pathways to, 8; as social justice, 82–83; transformational leadership in shaping pathways to, 11; urban crisis and pathways to, 19–25

Multiracial democracy, at Maricopa Community Colleges, 75–83; and chancellor's diversity initiative, 78; and diversity strategic plan, 78–79; and governing board statement on diversity, 78; and Maricopa Community Colleges' guiding principles, 78; and Maricopa Community Colleges' institutional values, 78; and Maricopa Community Colleges' mission statement, 77; and Maricopa Community Colleges' vision statement, 77; and recognizing community colleges as living laboratories for diversity and social justice, 79–80

Myran, G., 3, 4, 7, 14, 32, 33, 45, 79, 82, 93, 96

National Center for Education Statistics Integrated Postsecondary Data System, 69

National completeness initiatives, 22–23

National Council of Black American Affairs, 1

Nelson, T., 101

New Community College (Manhattan), 98

New community college business and finance model, 93–103; activating, 98–101; and community college strategic development framework, 95–97; and disruptive innovations, 97–98; and district design initiative, 101–102; infusing, with democratic values, 103; and jumping S-curve forces driving new business and finance model, 95; and lessons learned from for-profit colleges, 94; and new financial realities and social equity agenda, 94; and old community college business and finance model, 94–95; and perceptions of community college leaders, 100–101; program cost and review model for, 102–103

"New normal" college, 16

New York City Department for Economic Opportunity, 23

Newsweek magazine, 66

Northwestern Michigan College, 101

Norton, D. P., 96

Nunes, P., 95

Obama, B., 20, 31, 86, 100

O'Bannion, T., 101

OEDC. See Organisation for Economic Development and Cooperation (OEDC)

Ohio, 55, 59

Ohio State University, 22

Oliff, P., 85

Omi, M., 20

Open door: implementing promise of, 31–32; reinventing, 14

Open door college, 15

Operation Pedro Pan, 64

Opportunity Nation, 22

Orfield, G., 21

Organisation for Economic Development and Cooperation (OEDC), 68, 69

Padrón, E. J., 3, 63

Palacios, V., 85

Parents Involve in Community Schools v. Seattle School District No. 1, 21

Parsons, M. H., 3, 7, 27, 28

Pathology of despair, 11

Pathways to the Future (Wayne County Community College District), 48

Pennsylvania, 55

Peter, D. Hart Research Associates, 67

Phoenix, Arizona, 76

Pierce, F., 8

Polonio, N., 38

Population Studies Center (PSC), Institute for Social Research, University of Michigan, 48

powell, j., 20

Princeton University, 41

Program for International Student Assessment (PISA; OEDC), 68–69

Project Focus report, 1

PSC. See Population Studies Center (PSC), Institute for Social Research, University of Michigan

Racial formation, theory of, 20

Racial repression, new era of, 24–25

Ransom, T., 81

Reardon, S. F., 21

Reclaiming the American Dream initiative (American Association of Community Colleges), 12–14

Reece, J., 21

Reinventing the Open Door: Transformational Strategies for Community Colleges (Myran), 14

Resegregation, 21

Responding to the Crisis of Urban America (Detroit, Michigan), 48
Rhodes, R. A., 38, 41
Ricci v. DeStefano, 21
Rivera, C., 40
Rose, R., 57
Roueche, J. E., 52, 57
Roueche, S. D., 52

San Antonio, Texas, 38
San Jose City College (California), 11
Schilling, J., 94
Scholastic Aptitude Test (SAT), 69
Scott-Skillman, T., 97
S-curve, 95
Senge, P. M., 30
Sheets, R., 97
Shugart, S., 86
Siegel-Hawley, G., 21
Simone, B., 96
Sinclair Community College (Dayton, Ohio), 59
Smink, J., 56
Smith, N., 1, 2, 47
Soares, L., 97
Social equity college, 16
South Mountain Community College (Maricopa Community Colleges), 81
Spellings, M., 47
Spoon River College (Illinois), 28
St. Louis Community College, 51, 59–60; Workforce Solutions Group, 59
Stanford University, 21
State of Missouri Division of Workforce Development, 59
STEM careers, 3, 40, 58, 60–61
Strickland, Barlett v., 21
Sugrue, T., 19
Sykes, A., 1, 2

T. Rowe Price, 51
Thomas, R., Jr., 56
Thornton, J. S., 3, 55, 100
Transformational leadership, 11
Truman Commission Report, 38

University Business magazine, 91
University of California, Berkeley, 22
University of Florida, 64, 66
University of Maryland, 9
University of Michigan, 22, 48
University of South Florida, 64

University of the District of Columbia Community College (UDC-CC), 29–30
Univision, 71
Urban community college: future of, 7–17; increasing relevance of curricular and student services in, 63–72; milieu of, 8; and mission statements revealing new emphasis on service continuum, 11–12; and reframing "democracy's college," 16–17; and reimagining future, 12–13; student profile, 10–11; term, 8; and tomorrow's most promising alternatives, 15–16
Urban underclass theory, 19
U.S. Census Bureau, 55
U.S. Department of Education, 46, 72
U.S. Department of Labor Community-Based Job Training Program, 60
U.S. Department of Labor Trade Adjustment Assistance Community College and Career Training Grant, 51
U.S. National Center for Education Statistics, 10
U.S. News & World Report, 66

Valadez, J. R., 38, 41
Valencia Community College (Florida), 86
Vaughn, G. B., 42
VOICE Maricopa, 79
Voluntary Framework on Accountability (VFA; AACC), 100

Washington County (Maryland), 98
Wayne County Community College District (WCCD; Michigan), 11–12, 14, 21, 23, 48, 101, 102; District Design Initiative (DDI), 102; Pathways to the Future, 101; School for Social Progress, 21–22
WCCCD. *See* Wayne County Community College District (Michigan)
Weisman, I. A., 42
Wells, C., 30
Wessel, D., 60
West, C., 48
West Virginia, 55
WestEd, 31
Wheelan, B., 29
Winant, H., 20
Women's Leadership Group, 79
Woodland, C, 3, 27

Woodruff, M., 56

Workforce development: and commu-nity college middle-skill careers niche, 47; definitions of career education and, 46; emerging themes of career education and, 48–49; employability gap and community college role in, 45–53; and equity imperative, 47–48; and general education for knowledge workers, 50–51; linking, to social equity, 17; strategic innovations in, 49–50; traditional meaning of, 46

Workforce development college, 16

Year Up, 51, 52

Zeiss, T., 96